RESOLVING DISPUTES
WITHOUT GOING TO COURT

RESOLVING DISPUTES WITHOUT GOING TO COURT

A CONSUMER GUIDE TO ALTERNATIVE DISPUTE RESOLUTION

ANDREW FLOYER ACLAND

CENTURY
BUSINESS
BOOKS

Andrew Floyer Acland has asserted his rights under the Copyright, Designs and Patents Act, 1988, to be identified as the author of this work.
First published in the United Kingdom by Century Ltd
Random House, 20 Vauxhall Bridge Road, London SW1V 2SA

Random House Australia (Pty) Limited
20 Alfred Street, Milsons Point, Sydney
New South Wales 2061, Australia

Random House New Zealand Limited
18 Poland Road, Glenfield
Auckland 10, New Zealand

Random House South Africa (Pty) Limited
PO Box 337, Bergvlei, South Africa

Random House UK Limited Reg. No. 954009

Papers used by Random House UK Limited are natural, recyclable products made from wood grown in sustainable forests. The manufacturing processes conform to the environmental regulations of the country of origin.

Some of the ideas in this book were first discussed by the author in his book *A Sudden Outbreak of Common Sense*, published by Hutchinson Business Books in 1990.

ISBN 0 7126 7522 1

Typeset by Deltatype Ltd, Ellesmere Port, Cheshire
Printed and bound in Great Britain by Mackays of Chatham plc, Chatham, Kent

It must be considered that there is nothing more difficult to carry out, nor more doubtful of success, nor more dangerous to handle, than to initiate a new order of things. For the reformer has enemies in all those that profit by the old order, and only lukewarm defenders in all those who would profit by the new order, this luke-warmness arising . . . partly from the incredulity of mankind, who do not truly believe in anything new until they have had actual experience of it.

Niccolo Machiavelli, *The Prince*, 1513

Acknowledgments

This book would not have been possible without the contributions, witting and unwitting, of hundreds of people: clients, colleagues, students, friends and relatives. I am enormously grateful to all of them, especially to those whom I shall never be able to thank in person for the experiences on which this book is based.

It could not have been written at all, however, without the help of friends and colleagues from ADR Group, the Centre for Dispute Resolution, National Family Mediation, the Family Mediators Association, Mediation UK, and Environmental Resolve. Thank you for your enthusiasm and support. I owe a particular debt of thanks to Andrew Fraley and Hermione Legg, who laboured through an early draft and made many invaluable suggestions; and to Lucy and Toby, who keep me going and know when not to interrupt.

The errors, misjudgments and infelicities are entirely mine.

Contents

Introduction

How to Use This Book

There is an old Chinese curse: '*May you have a lawsuit in which you know you are right.*' This book is not about the rights and wrongs of disputes: but about the *results*. The purpose of this book is to help you – whether as an individual, or as the representative of a business, a local authority, a voluntary organization, or a government department – to resolve all types of dispute as quickly, amicably and cost-effectively as possible. Its purpose is to help you stay out of court – and, in some cases, with appropriate advice, avoid legal processes altogether.

This is what many people seem to want from a modern justice system. Time and again, people tell me that they do not want to go through a trial. More than this, they say they cannot understand the law and the legal system with all its complicated language and quaint procedures, and they have little faith in either its fairness or its efficiency as a means of resolving disputes. They resent the high costs, the endless delays, the tottering heaps of paper which take over their lives. Instead, people want something much simpler: a process conducted in plain language, based on common sense, and geared to getting problems sorted out round a table rather than in the hothouse atmosphere of the courtroom.

More and more people are reaching this conclusion – from prominent business people to lawyers themselves. They recognize that the law, in practice if not in intention, is a lottery. You may get what you want; equally, you may find yourself haemorrhaging time, energy and money. Unless you are poor enough to qualify for legal aid (and these days that means very poor indeed), rich, legally insured, or you are representing a large organization with considerable resources, going to law to settle any dispute is liable to be ruinous. Whether it be a boundary dispute with a neighbour, a

1

contract dispute with another company, or a disputed claim with your insurance company, ending up in court could cost you more than the case is worth.

Until recently, though, you had little option. It was the old problem of *fight* or *flight*. Grit your teeth, gird your loins, and get stuck in; or just grit your teeth and walk away – sacrificing your pride and your rights because the costs and risks of defending them were too high.

This book describes some other options which have recently become available for dealing with all sorts of disputes. Collectively they are known as *Alternative Dispute Resolution*, ADR for short, because they are alternatives to the traditional processes used by the law. Of the ADR alternatives on offer, by far the most widely used is *mediation*, because it is the most straightforward, flexible and effective of ADR processes. As increasing numbers of people are beginning to discover, mediation is not just for international diplomats or for sorting out industrial relations problems. It can help resolve anything from a bust-up with a partner to a planning dispute, from a spat with the neighbours to who gets the microwave when your marriage comes unstuck.

While most of the book focuses on commercial and legal disputes, it ends with a review of how else mediation is being used: as an alternative to long and costly public inquiries; as a tool for community participation in making complex environmental decisions; as a means to help families to sort out separation and divorce, victims to meet offenders, and neighbours to resolve their differences.

So, whoever you are, before you ask your solicitor to write nasty letters or issue writs, discuss with them whether to try mediation. If they dismiss it out of hand (or worse, have never heard of mediation or ADR) you would be best advised to find another solicitor. It may mean they are more concerned about their interests than yours, or else completely out of touch. In fact, in future they will probably *have* to discuss ADR with you. While this book was being written Lord Woolf, who was asked by the Lord Chancellor to review our system of civil justice in March 1994, published his Interim Report, *Access to Justice*. One of his recommendations is that people going to court 'should be required to state whether the question of ADR has been discussed and, if not, why not'. He also says that a judge 'should be able to take into account the litigant's unreasonable refusal to attempt ADR'. (*Access to Justice,* Chapter 18, Rec. 9 & 10.)

Most of the books which have so far been written about ADR are designed for lawyers, academics, or for people who practise as mediators. They tend to use a lot of technical jargon, or are written in a way which puts off those who can most benefit from ADR – people who have disputes. I know what this sort of writing is like for people outside the field: it is how I feel when I am trying to understand the manual which came with my computer.

This book is not intended for lawyers or mediators or academics: it is for consumers. Having said that, I hope it will also be useful for those who practise ADR – whether solicitors and barristers sitting beside clients during a mediation, or for the person who is mediating. At the very least, it might help remind them that ADR should be led by the needs of its customers rather than driven by the interests of its practitioners.

While it is designed to tell you as much as possible about ADR, I hope it will mostly be used to help people who are caught in a dispute and do not want to end up in court. You can read it straight through, of course, but it is more likely you will pick it off the shelf when you want to be reminded of something, or to contact an ADR provider, or when you are preparing a case for mediation and need a checklist of what to do. In any such book there has to be balance between clarity and comprehensiveness. I am biased towards clarity. I believe it is more important for you to have a good grasp of what ADR is, how it works, and how to make the most of the opportunities it offers, than it is to drown you in theory and detail. One of the purposes of ADR is, after all, to make resolving disputes easier.

The book is divided into three parts:

Part One, Alternative Dispute Resolution, Chapters 1–5, is an overview of ADR and mediation: what it is, where it comes from, the basis of how it works.

Part Two, Making the Most of Mediation, Chapters 6–14, describes mediation stage by stage, covering the issues most commonly asked about mediation:

– when, and when not, to use mediation
– how to prepare for mediation

- what mediation sessions are like
- what to do during mediation.

Part Three, Where to Find Your Mediator, Chapters 15–19, describes the various organizations in the field, what sort of mediation they provide, and how to contact them if you think you might want to use mediation:

- in legal and commercial disputes
- in separation and divorce
- to resolve a dispute with a neighbour
- to build consensus in a public policy dispute
- to prevent and resolve disputes within or between organizations.

Finally, Chapter 20 provides a short review of Lord Woolf's recommendations in relation to ADR, and speculates briefly on where ADR may be going over the next few years.

★ ★ ★

Throughout the book, but especially in Part Two, you will find two types of text: CORE and COMMENT.

CORE is text wrapped in a box. It usually contains:
- a few bullet points;
- a summary;
- something concise and worth remembering when you are actually involved in a dispute.

COMMENT is the rest of the text. It provides examples of mediation in action, reflections on the subjects in the chapter, and general discussion of how mediation works and what to do in specific situations. Although the book is designed to be informative, I have tried throughout to stick to what you really need to know in order to make your mediation a success. I have severely limited the use of anecdotes, examples and case studies, because every dispute is different, and it is more important to read the book with your own problem in mind.

There are three more points I should make. First this book is designed to be realistic rather than idealistic. There are no foolproof means to resolve problems between people: if there were, neither mediation nor the whole, complicated paraphernalia of the law would be necessary. Mediation is not always suitable, and it cannot always work – any more than using the law is appropriate in every situation. The best reason for understanding mediation and how it works is that it widens the range of options open to you.

Second, this book is only the starting point. If you are involved in any sort of dispute, and having read the book you think mediation might be able to help, contact the most appropriate of the organizations mentioned in Part Three and talk to someone about your specific situation. Do not try to set up your own mediation using a friend or a relative as the mediator. It is a skilled role and people need to be trained to do it. The organizations featured here all run networks of mediators and should be able to find someone to suit your situation, location, and pocket.

Third, this is not a real 'consumer's guide' in that I have made no attempt to make judgments about the various organizations in the field. As there is as yet no central register, it is not possible even to list them all. Neither have I attempted mediation's equivalent of Michelin Stars: it would be pointless because it is the individual mediators who determine the quality of a mediation, and there is no way to know or judge them all. Having said that, all the organizations mentioned here have systems for training and supervising mediators, which offer you some assurance of quality.

Finally, please let me know whether you have found this book useful and what else you would like to see in it.

Andrew Floyer Acland
Foxcote
Gloucestershire
June 1995

PART ONE:

Alternative Dispute Resolution

Chapter 1

What's the Problem?

The problem, in a nutshell, is that most people, faced with a dispute, want to settle it as quickly, as amicably and as cheaply as they possibly can. Our culture and our legal system, on the other hand, are *adversarial*: they work on the basis of right or wrong, win or lose, either/or. Moreover, the law, our principal system for resolving disputes, is not only adversarial, it is slow, expensive and user-unfriendly. Even when we want to agree, the way the law actually works often results in driving us further apart rather than bringing us together. And even when the law is not directly involved, it tends to influence how we approach conflict and disputes.

THE ADVERSARIAL APPROACH

The classic example of this, which you will hear up and down the land from the smartest drawing-rooms of Belgravia to the humblest council flats, is in a divorce case. '*It was all perfectly amicable,*' we hear time and again, '*until the lawyers got involved.*' Now, this is not altogether, and not always, fair to the lawyers. It is not just the law which is the problem; the law is a reflection of how our entire culture works. And even if our culture was less adversarial, individual people would still pick fights; not everybody does want to reach a fast and amicable agreement. Sometimes people want a fight in order to justify themselves, to get what they want, or simply for the satisfaction of seeing the other person beaten and humiliated. Some people just like a good fight. Or that is what they want at the beginning. After a few months or years, though, even the most implacable of fighters may find themselves wishing it was all over.

9

If we set aside our adversarial culture, and the people who like fighting, there are still reasons we human beings find it difficult to reach agreement. Face-to-face negotiation can be extremely difficult if the situation involves our pride, our vital interests, or our principles. However much we want to agree, the circumstances may make it very difficult to do so and the civil legal system has evolved in part as a response to this. Recognizing how hard it can be for people to agree, the law – based on Acts of Parliament and on precedent, what judges have ruled in the past – sets out a framework of what it means to be 'right' in any situation, and provides a system for working out who is 'right', and therefore who should 'win'. So far, so good. Law does, after all, underpin what we call civilization.

The problems come both in the way the law sets out to discover who is 'right', and what it then does as a result. The first problem stems from this anxiety to prove that one side is 'right' and the other 'wrong'. In many situations there may be a right and wrong – at least in the eyes of the law. And if the establishment of right and wrong, truth and falsehood, is important, then the adversarial process is a very good way to achieve it. But in many other situations there is a misunderstanding, a failure of communication, a clash of values, a collision of equally valid interests. In these the problem is not that people are right or wrong, but that they are *different;* they want different things and are heading in different directions. In this sort of situation the adversarial right-or-wrong approach of the law can be largely irrelevant. Worse, it may encourage people to focus on what separates them, rather than on any common ground there is or could be.

Take the divorce situation. Each person has a range of needs, interests, fears and concerns. Because the law is adversarial, and lawyers are trained to think adversarially, each side's lawyers will push their client's interests – that is what they are paid to do – and will try to play down or even denigrate the needs and interests of the other side. How they do this depends on the lawyer and the situation, but quite frequently it means veiled threats, verbal bullying, digging up past differences, or just refusing to communicate.

The purpose is to use every means possible to get the upper hand. In the course of this, not surprisingly, relations between those involved tend to deteriorate even further, both sides feel threatened, and what happens? Everybody digs in and prepares to do battle. So the *process* of the law can actually encourage people to fight – even if they do not want to. This predicament is particularly unfortunate in divorce cases because there is often one indisputable piece of common ground: the desire of both parents to safeguard the interests of their children.

The same points can equally be applied to problems in a professional partnership or arising from a contract dispute. Whatever the situation, using an adversarial process to resolve a fight can be rather like trying to put out a bonfire with petrol.

Origins of the Adversarial Approach

It is easy to blame the lawyers, but the roots of this problem probably go way back to Western methods of argument developed many centuries ago. In his book *Conflicts: A Better Way to Resolve Them,* Edward de Bono, the inventor of 'lateral thinking', argues that it was the mediaeval theologians who got us into this mess. They needed a powerful method to repel heretics and so refined a way of thinking which proved you were either a believer or not: no room for quibblers or agnostics. De Bono contrasts this with, for example, the Japanese approach, which put more emphasis on respect and manners, and made it very rude to contradict someone. As disagreement was very difficult, people put all their efforts into finding ways to agree. This, says De Bono, may explain why the Americans (where the adversarial system has become something of an art form) have one lawyer for every two or three hundred people, and the Japanese one for every nine *thousand.*

Whatever its origins, this is the nature of our culture, and of the legal system which has evolved within it. Blaming the lawyers is rather like blaming the messenger for the message. This adversarial culture and the adversarial legal system is so much taken for granted by lawyers and by us, their clients, that often it seems not to occur to any of us to resolve disputes any other way. I recently mediated a divorce, for example, in which both sides were desperate to reach a settlement without going to court. One of the lawyers, however, was on the train which chugs steadily to a court hearing, and the possibility of getting off along the way was just not on his ticket or timetable. Many attempts to meet and talk about settlement – over a period of *two years* – had failed. It was simply not a priority for him, and until somebody suggested mediation neither the husband nor wife, nor the other solicitor involved, thought they had any alternative but to chug with him all the way to the trial.

Costs and Consequences of the Adversarial Approach

The job of lawyers is basically to solve problems, and that is what most of them set out to do. They will tell you that they always set out to be conciliatory and negotiate a settlement. Indeed, in many cases they succeed. It is difficult to get any firm figures, but most lawyers agree that over 95 per cent of all civil and commercial cases are settled out of court. In other words, they argue, lawyers are good at negotiating settlements, and their clients ending up in court is a sign of failure for them as much as for the clients. This is all fine, except that the process of getting to settlement may currently take years, cost a fortune, increasingly exclude the clients because they cannot understand what is going on, and the stresses and strains of it all can ruin lives. And that is before you consider the cases which do not settle, and are fought to a finish in court.

It is right and proper that some cases should go before a judge, and in a later chapter these sorts of cases will be clearly described. It is also fair to say that in some cases people are so far apart that negotiating an agreement is impossible: they would rather take their chances at trial. This is not necessarily the lawyers' fault. If we create an adversarial culture, then we have to expect that some people will behave adversarially even when it may not be appropriate to do so.

It is also true, however, that large numbers of cases drag on far longer than necessary before being settled in a way which could have been agreed months or years previously. Some cases are abandoned in the course of a trial, leaving each side to pay their costs without having gained any benefit apart from learning that the risks of losing are too great. For those who settle at the door of the court, meanwhile, there is the irritation of knowing that they have paid a large fee to a barrister, to say nothing of thousands of pounds in solicitors' fees preparing for an event which ultimately never happens.

Worse still, there is the case which is clearly won, but the winner ends up paying more in costs than the victory achieved. Still more horrible is the victory which means nothing because it turns out that the loser has in the meantime gone bankrupt. These are, do not forget, the superficial results. Many cases, both successful and unsuccessful, impose enormous strains on both sides, their invisible costs measured in illness, strained relationships and lost opportunities.

* * *

In summary, we have landed ourselves with a culture and a legal system which conspire to discourage agreement even when it may be possible and desirable. In an ideal world we would have a society in which everybody is upright, honest and truthful; in which there is neither greed, nor selfishness, nor power-mania; in which all disputes, if there is anything left to dispute about, are resolved immediately and without a trace of anger, rancour, or recrimination. As this is not going to happen short of the Second Coming, the least we can do is offer people the best opportunities to make agreement possible if that is what they want. We should provide a system which brings people together, rather than driving them apart, and which encourages the sort of behaviour which leads to reconciliation rather than further division.

ALTERNATIVE DISPUTE RESOLUTION

Reconciliation is what Alternative Dispute Resolution is all about. I used to argue that the word *Alternative* had off-putting connotations. I thought a more sober *A*, such as *Appropriate*, would help advocates of ADR fit more easily into our cynical age. It would also help us to explain that we do not totally reject the adversarial system – as I've said, it has its uses – it is just that it is not always appropriate in every case, any more than it is always appropriate to use an alternative. As I have travelled the country, talking to business people, community organizations, solicitors, barristers and anybody else interested in finding better ways to deal with disputes, I have found that people really *do* want an alternative. As the alternative is additional to the current system, and often more appropriate to people's real needs, the word has become more a source of pride than embarrassment.

The Origins of ADR

So where does the notion of Alternative Dispute Resolution come from? Like much else that we now take for granted and have made our own, it originated in the United States of America. In the late 1970s people there became increasingly concerned about the costs and delays of the legal system, and the knock-on effect these had on everything from insurance premiums to general consumer costs. America is also a notoriously litigious society: we have all heard horror stories about people claiming millions over apparently trivial issues. Some of these are no doubt exaggerated, but the threat of being taken to court in America is serious enough for people to carry heavy insurance against it.

Towards the end of the 1970s a few brave souls began to think about ways of cutting short the legal process. The first efforts at this seem to have concentrated on making trials less of a nightmare. Why not, they reasoned, have private trials at a time and a place chosen by the clients rather than the State? If that meant hiring a private judge for the day: well, why not? Private judging has always been controversial. The process is not open to scrutiny, but it is, in theory at least, open to all kinds of abuse and corruption, and serious allegations are made about it from time to time.

Besides, this and various other ways of expediting the court process did not address the key problem: the time and cost involved in getting cases to trial, and the fact that most of them were settled before trial anyway. The obvious answer was to get negotiations going sooner, and make them work better. And what do we do these days if we want something to work better, but cannot do it ourselves? Exactly: we hire a consultant. Only the consultant in the case of a dispute happens to be called a *mediator*. It is important to realize that the mediator's job is not to behave like a judge or arbitrator and decide the case according to who is right or wrong, but simply to help the people in dispute to negotiate their own settlement. The role of the mediator, and the way it returns the power of decision to those who 'own' the problem, explains much of the success of the ADR movement.

And it has become a success. In a recent survey conducted by the Society of Professionals in Dispute Resolution, 82 per cent of Americans, once they had had some minimal education about ADR, said they would be likely to use an ADR process rather than go to court. I would be cautious about taking such a figure too

14

literally, but it does suggest that many people are at least open to the idea of doing things differently. For example, in mid-1993 the *Wall Street Journal* reported that some 40,000 civil cases were resolved by the four main American ADR providers. Given that mediation is by definition a private process and goes unreported, and that much of it is done by individuals, it is impossible to know the true figure for the number of cases being mediated rather than litigated.

I have heard it estimated that alternative means are being used to resolve as much as 20 per cent of all American litigation. Indeed, it has become so common that 'alternative' is hardly appropriate any more. As an attorney friend in San Francisco commented to me recently (he had been to mediation with four cases that month alone), ADR is becoming the norm and the courts are increasingly regarded as the eccentric alternative for the very rich, the very poor, or the very masochistic.

ADR has taken root in the United States. It is being used for everything from settling insurance claims and sexual harassment cases to resolving disputes between universities and their students, farmers and agricultural money lenders, old people's homes and the families of the residents. Banks have ADR clauses in credit card agreements with their customers; most of the Fortune 500 companies are pledged to use ADR rather than litigation wherever possible; in 1990 the American government passed two Administrative Dispute Resolution Acts which basically state that every federal agency must use ADR to save the taxpayer money.

Resolving disputes is important work, but it is not the end of ADR. People are beginning to realize that techniques which help to resolve a dispute amicably may *prevent it ever happening in the first place*. So federal and state government departments, corporations, voluntary organizations, universities and just about anybody with any initiative, are beginning to experiment and use mediation and other ADR processes to achieve agreement about anything from the route of a new road to the details of new government regulations on broadcasting. In fact, ADR processes are increasingly being used in any situation where people recognize that they can achieve more by working together collaboratively than they can by working separately, and perhaps adversarially.

In short, in the United States people are using ADR methods to do anything which will benefit from agreement rather than disagreement. Do they still disagree? Of course. Is there still litigation? You bet: about 18 *million* new lawsuits meander through the legal system annually. It is big business, and ADR is only just beginning to make a dent in the expenses and delays suffered by many litigants. Even so, the Centre for Public Resources in New York reported in February 1995 that business disputes involving some $1.5 *billion* had been successfully resolved using ADR in the previous year. A survey of 109 companies which brought disputes to CPR estimated direct legal cost savings in excess of $75.5 million.

Where are the lawyers in all this? Surely they cannot be happy with anything which threatens their livelihoods? Interestingly, many of the people who are driving ADR are lawyers themselves because they recognize that it offers new opportunities for them to render valuable services to their clients. As with most new technology, it does not have to mean that jobs are destroyed; it *does* mean that those who are flexible enough to adapt first tend to profit most from the change.

ADR in the United Kingdom

The first commercial ADR company, IDR (International Dispute Resolution) Europe was launched in 1989. In 1990 the non-profit Centre for Dispute Resolution (CEDR) was established with the blessing of the Confederation of British Industry and backed by many of our biggest legal, accountancy and commercial names. In the five or so years since then, these two organizations have demonstrated that ADR works here as well as it does in the United States. This should have come as no surprise, because while the use of ADR in legal and commercial cases is relatively novel, it has been successfully used to resolve industrial, matrimonial and neighbourhood disputes for very much longer.

National Family Mediation, formerly the National Family Conciliation Council, was established in 1981, and has since helped many thousands of divorcing couples to resolve the outstanding issues between them. Likewise, Mediation UK, formerly the Forum for Initiatives in Mediation and Reparation, has pioneered the use of mediation in communities and within the criminal justice system. More recently, people here have been experimenting with consensus-building and other processes which fall under the general heading of ADR. The Environment Council, for example, is having some success in persuading

16

government departments, local authorities, businesses and voluntary organizations that mediation and consensus-building should begin to complement our more traditional planning and consultative procedures.

Finally, we should mention the government in all this. What does the government think of ADR? It seems to like it. The Department of Environment has supported the use of mediation to deal with the most common reason for disputes between neighbours: noise. In March 1995, Robert Atkins MP, then Minister for the Environment and Countryside, commented, 'As far as central government and public bodies are concerned, mediation is being considered as an option in many areas.' He went on to mention the use of mediation in many different contexts, and government funding for research into its cost-effectiveness as an alternative to more formal methods of dispute resolution. Meanwhile, in a recent CBI/CEDR publication the then President of the Board of Trade, Michael Heseltine, welcomed the potential benefits of ADR to industry, and commented that his department was working to raise company awareness of ADR processes. This is encouraging, and it will be even more so when we see more cases in which the government is involved being mediated.

Lord Woolf and *Access to Justice*

The final stamp of ADR's respectability arrived in June 1995 when Lord Woolf published his Interim Report, *Access to Justice*. He was asked by the Lord Chancellor in March 1994 to review the civil justice system. To the delight of all who have campaigned for the increased use of ADR, Lord Woolf devoted an entire chapter of his Report to this subject, and was generous in his assessment both of its main ideas and its supporters. He comments that there is worldwide interest in ADR and it deserves careful monitoring by the Judicial Studies Board, and recommends that the Judiciary and the Court Service in general should become better acquainted with the whole subject. While he stops short of recommending the direct annexing of ADR to the current court system – his other recommendations already amount to several revolutions in current practice – throughout his Report there is an awareness of the ADR's potential contribution to improving British justice.

* * *

It would be wrong to end this first chapter without commenting briefly on where ADR may go. It is becoming increasingly clear that there are two main streams of thought and practice within the ADR movement. For one stream, ADR is simply a cost-effective alternative to litigation. For the other stream, ADR has a philosophical and even religious dimension, and its purpose is to help people break free of the adversarial traditions which contribute to so many of our problems. For this latter stream, a true ADR process provides emancipation from subservience to higher authority, and encourages and enables people to take control of their own lives and responsibility for their own actions in responding to conflict, the most demanding of human situations. Finally, some people see in it also the first stirrings of a more profound transformation in how we deal with our differences in needs, values, and cultures.

The division into two streams was brought home to me by a senior barrister who has been much involved in the law's response to ADR. He said words to the effect that, as far as he was concerned, mediation and arbitration are much the same thing, because people always need someone older and wiser to tell them what to do. It is little wonder that many people in the more reflective stream of ADR are deeply wary of the damage which too much legal involvement could do to the wider purposes of ADR. For the moment, our inclination is inclusive: to bring the lawyers on board along with governments and corporations. This is also pragmatic: it will be much easier to gain acceptance for ADR from the inside out, than try to shoulder aside the institutions which control how people handle conflict.

ADR can be deeply subversive – but not in that it wastes its energies on shouting and bombing, and thereby simply reproduces the tendencies which it purports to dislike. Its aim is to subvert the depressingly persistent habits of human conflict which impose such suffering and hardship. There will still be a need for determined advocacy wherever there is injustice, and of course ADR is no panacea for every human ill. But if it reduces the cost of conflict for even a few thousand people every year, freeing them to do better things with their time and money, then it will be serving its purpose.

Chapter 2

The Alternatives in Alternative Dispute Resolution

Many people have by now heard of Alternative Dispute Resolution, but few really know what it entails. There have been some books on the subject and, if you are a lawyer, a business executive or other professional, you may well belong to one of the burgeoning ADR networks. But if you are none of these, or you only skip through the legal and business pages of the papers, you could well have missed any reference to ADR. The purpose of this chapter is to describe the main ADR processes and clear up some of the common confusions about them.

While some forward-thinking people in business and the professions have done much to welcome and spread the gospel of ADR, relatively little has been done to make consumers aware of its potential benefits. This is not due to any deliberate conspiracy; even the Law Society, the guardian of legal privilege and responsibility, has been an enthusiastic proponent of ADR. Indeed, not long ago it announced that ADR was likely to be one of the key growth areas for the legal profession in the 1990s. The cynics may regard this as the early kiss of death. Meanwhile, argue the cautious, until we know what ADR processes can do, we should be wary of offering them to the consumer in the street.

Well, we already know what a nightmare litigation can be but nobody suggests not offering *that* to the consumer, and thousands of people continue to be dragged through unnecessary and unwelcome legal proceedings because they are not aware of any alternative. In short, the time has come to take the wraps off ADR, so this chapter begins with descriptions of the main ADR processes, and goes on to consider the particular challenges and contrasts they are making to how law is practised. We consider the response of the legal profession to ADR, the specific recommendations made by Lord Woolf in his *Access to Justice* Report, and consumer experience of ADR so far.

Running through the book as a whole, you may detect my concern to trample only delicately on legal toes. The consumer reading this may well wonder why the legal profession is not skewered and grilled as thoroughly as it sometimes deserves. The lawyer reading it may feel that legal considerations are not accorded due weight. The point to make here is that there is an honest tension between advocating the use of ADR wherever appropriate as an alternative to legal processes, and encouraging lawyers to see it as an opportunity rather than a threat.

THE MAIN ADR PROCESSES

Mediation

Alternative Dispute Resolution is an umbrella term. When people talk about using ADR in this country they almost always mean *mediation*, the most commonly used process, which is why this book concentrates on it. Mediation is the ADR process which is most likely to be of interest to most people for the foreseeable future. (I use the term mediation, by the way, to mean both mediation and *conciliation*. I have never seen a convincing definition of the difference, and there is anyway a growing tendency to use mediation to cover both.) For now, it is enough to summarize mediation as a means of assisting people to negotiate: an independent mediator brings those in dispute together and through a mixture of joint and private meetings, helps them work out their own negotiated solution. Sounds simple and obvious? It is: but it can also be an extraordinarily complex and subtle process demanding skills of a high order.

Consensus-building

If mediation is the most widely used ADR process, the next most significant is probably *consensus-building,* which is used to resolve complex, multi-issue problems. Basically, it is multi-lateral mediation: a method of finding common ground when there are many different people and interests involved in a situation. For example, it has been used to help people resolve planning controversies, and it is likely to be used more frequently as local councils, government agencies and private organizations grapple with the need to achieve some consensus and commitment to implementing potentially controversial environmental policies. In such situations you might find the local tourist board, consumer groups, sports clubs, commercial enterprises and conservationists all battling over what should happen. The more complex the situation, the more important it is to design a process which can address the needs and interests of all concerned, and produce the best possible outcome for as many people as possible.

Joint Fact-finding and Independent Expert Appraisal

Consensus-building will often involve other ADR processes, particularly mediation and *joint fact-finding* or *independent expert appraisal*. These are also stand-alone ADR processes used to assist negotiations in any context where the facts of a situation are disputed, or where the opinion of an independent expert might help to nudge negotiations towards settlement. Rather than paying rival experts to produce rival versions of what is 'right', or each side setting out to prove that its version of the facts is 'true', people agree in advance to accept the findings of an independent expert, or work together to come up with a joint survey of the facts of a case. This tends to generate light rather than just heat, and is usually much cheaper than each side commissioning its own experts and then arguing over their findings.

As stand-alone processes, independent expert appraisal and joint fact-finding can be useful in, for example, a contested insurance case. It may prove cost-effective to commission a joint fact-finding process to establish the loss involved, but then return to the normal adversarial process to argue liability – or possibly the other way round. This illustrates a general principle of ADR: you design the process to fit the needs of those who have the problem. Unlike the litigation process, you do not simply cram the problem into a single established process regardless of whether that process is appropriate.

Executive Tribunal or 'Mini-Trial'

Another ADR process you are likely to come across over the next few years is the *executive tribunal* or *mini-trial*. The executive tribunal enables senior executives of organizations in dispute to assess a situation as objectively as possible before directly negotiating a solution. This process can be used where legal departments or other staff have become bogged down in a dispute which seems to be going nowhere, is costing time and money, and damaging other parts of a commercial relationship. The process begins with a formal presentation by those directly involved in the case to a panel consisting of a neutral chair and a senior, perhaps the most senior, executive of each organization. Ideally these executives will not previously have been involved in the case.

Following the formal presentations, the panel will ask questions to clarify any points or challenge particular arguments. They will then retire to a private room and with the help of the neutral panel chair they will attempt to negotiate a solution. The role of the chair in an executive tribunal is similar to that of a mediator. This process is sometimes called a 'mini-trial' because in the use of formal presentations and the questioning of witnesses and experts for each side, it resembles a 'proper' trial. The crucial difference is that the aim is voluntary agreement rather than a win-lose outcome imposed by a third party such as a judge or arbitrator.

Non-binding Adjudication

In *non-binding adjudication* a third party hears the arguments and then gives an opinion either on the case as a whole or on a particular aspect of it. This can help the parties to appreciate what may happen should the case proceed to trial, or it may be used just to help get them past a particular point which is obstructing progress in negotiations. There are also situations in which both parties may find it useful to agree to accept adjudication as a temporarily binding decision until, for example, other procedures are completed or other events take place. They may then decide to reach a voluntary settlement, or seek a legally binding adjudication through litigation or arbitration.

Dispute Systems Design

An ADR process gaining in popularity across the Atlantic is the somewhat cumbersomely named *Dispute Systems Design* (DSD), which is used to prevent or resolve conflict within organizations or within a pattern of relationships. Dispute Systems Design has two thrusts. The first is to help people change the way they currently handle disputes so that disagreements can be resolved more rapidly and more amicably, and with the least damage to the organization, system or network in which they occur. The second thrust is to prevent disputes arising in the first place, and to train people to resolve their differences before they turn into actual disputes. The practical impact of DSD is to improve working practices and working relations so as to reduce the need for litigation and referrals to industrial or administrative tribunals.

Dispute Systems Design is probably the most under-used of ADR processes, but potentially one of the most significant. After all, the more disputes can be prevented, the less you need the other processes; and however expensive it is to prevent conflict, it is almost invariably cheaper than having to pick up the pieces after it. For this reason, and although it contradicts my intention to concentrate on mediation, it is discussed in more detail in chapter 18.

The legal profession is already heavily involved in dispute prevention: one has only to think of the care, for example, which competent solicitors take in drafting wills or contracts. The aim is to make everything so crystal clear, in both law and effect, that nothing can be misunderstood or be open to later question and dispute. Much of the time this is happily achieved. There is also an awful lot of poor drafting which positively encourages misunderstanding. Even if there were not, a skilful lawyer can often find some technical way around the most carefully drafted form of words.

Preventing disputes requires more than good legal drafting. It is about creating patterns of relationships and interests which are self-regulating, even self-reinforcing, so that nobody has any motive to get into a dispute. This means, for example, designing a relationship so that if anything goes wrong there is an accepted mechanism for dealing with it which both parties have a powerful incentive to make work. This is the province of Dispute Systems Design.

PROCESSES SOMETIMES DESCRIBED AS ADR

There is a no man's land where ADR purists and ADR pragmatists debate what can properly be regarded as ADR, and what should not. It is interesting to note that Lord Woolf in *Access to Justice* does not appear always to make such distinctions. For example, he quotes *arbitration* as the first form of ADR, which it is in the sense that it is an alternative to going to court, but it is not regarded as an ADR process by ADR purists, for reasons I will explain in a moment. Lord Woolf also includes *ombudsmen* and *administrative tribunals* as ADR processes. He admits the latter are not a form of ADR in the sense of an additional option available to parties in dispute since their jurisdiction normally excludes that of the courts. He points out that they are, however, 'intended to provide a simpler, less formal and more accessible means of resolving certain types of dispute than through the normal court process'.

The debate about what is, and what is not ADR is crystallized by the question of whether *arbitration* is an ADR process. For the non-legal reader, arbitration is a sort of trial in which the decision, or award, is made not by a judge, but by an impartial lawyer or expert in the particular field of the case who has been trained to arbitrate. Should arbitration be regarded as an ADR process? In the sense that it is an alternative to litigation, then it probably should be. But many people question the inclusion of arbitration on the ADR menu, for three principal reasons.

First, arbitration is generally as lengthy and as expensive as litigation, so it fails one of the primary aims of ADR which is to make dispute resolution cheaper and easier for the consumer. Indeed, Lord Woolf himself quotes the common description of arbitration as 'litigation behind closed doors', and the perception that it is 'no quicker or cheaper than litigation because it has become over-dominated by court procedures'. Rejection on these grounds may be modified as more ADR providers offer 'fast track' or 'documents-only arbitration', which aim to reduce both costs and complexity. It has to be said, though, that in practice it is difficult to streamline any adversarial process without damaging perceptions of its fairness. Lord Woolf uses arbitration as a warning of the possible consequences if other forms of ADR are allowed to become too institutionalized.

Second, one of the main characteristics of the true ADR process is that *the results of the process are determined by the parties themselves*, and not by any third party – however impartial or expert he or she may be. This is the main reason why arbitration, ombudsmen and all sorts of decision-making tribunals tend to be rejected as ADR processes.

Third, arbitration is an adversarial process, so it fails what might be called the 'moral imperative' behind ADR: that a dispute resolution process should be designed to bring people together rather than to thrust them apart.

For the purists, the difference between arbitration and a true ADR process becomes apparent when one compares arbitration and mediation. The two are often confused, much to the despair of mediators, and this is perhaps the point to describe the crucial differences before describing mediation more fully in the next chapter. The confusion arises because arbitration is a well-known alternative to litigation, and the arbitrator is also a neutral third party. But there the similarity ends. The job of the arbitrator is to listen to the evidence and the arguments from both sides, and then to make a decision as to what should happen. In contrast, the mediator has no power or authority to make a decision, and should resist the temptation even to offer an opinion on the issues. The job of the mediator is to help people come to their own decisions and negotiate their own agreements.

* * *

ADR, THE LAW AND CONSUMERS

We can approach the tricky relationship between ADR and the law from three angles. First, we need to examine the key contrasts between legal and ADR processes; second, we can look at the legal response to ADR; and third, offer an overview of where ADR can particularly benefit consumers.

ADR and Legal Processes: Key Differences

This section carries a small health warning for lawyer readers, though I hope none of it is gratuitously insulting. It simply reflects what I have heard from people in the course of my work. The differences described here do not imply that lawyers do not or cannot share ADR's approach. It is more that the practice of law does not always allow or encourage it.

Law	ADR
Adversarial	Non-adversarial

Lawyers tend to approach disputes adversarially even before it is necessary, and regardless of the situation and the circumstances. This is hardly surprising: it is what they are trained to do. But it may not always be the best approach. The adversarial assumption and what ADR does about it is covered in detail in Chapter 4.

Law	ADR
Deals with situation as defined by law	Deals with situation as it is on the ground

Some lawyers seem to get so involved in how the law describes a situation, and the intellectual challenges that poses, that they lose touch with the personal or commercial realities of it. This is how it sometimes happens that people end up spending more in legal fees than they can ever hope to recover. ADR aims always to be realistic: in fact mediators sometimes describe themselves as 'agents of reality'.

Law	ADR
Legally (producer)–driven	Consumer-led

It is fair to say that in recent years the legal profession has become much more commercially aware, but there are still some lawyers who seem to regard sordid commercial realities as rather beneath them. I have also come across some who are quite happy to pursue a legal action in the comfortable knowledge that, whatever happens, they will get paid. Being consumer-led, ADR has value for money as a prime objective. A successful commercial mediation lasting eight hours should not cost more than about £1,500 at the outside.

Law	ADR
Uses legal language, which tends to obstruct communication	Uses ordinary, everyday language to make communication as clear and effective as possible

When I was involved in training conciliators working for the Solicitors Complaints Bureau, it did not surprise me to discover that a large percentage of complaints stem from the failure of solicitors to communicate adequately with their clients or with each other, and from the tone in which they do so. The first job in any ADR process is to improve communications. Also, being consumer-led, ADR starts from a rather different attitude to clients

Further communications problems are caused by the way our language is murdered in the name of 'legal accuracy'. Perhaps. And perhaps it is just another way of preserving the aura of magic and special knowledge with which some lawyers like to surround themselves. Too often legal language serves to confuse and obscure and creates problems rather than prevents them. ADR processes are conducted in plain English: and should those present be tempted into legalese they will immediately be asked to translate. In handling sensitive situations absolute clarity of communication is vital.

Law	ADR
Training in law	Training in negotiation and mediation

The lack of negotiation training for lawyers continues to astound me: it is, after all, something most lawyers can be more or less guaranteed to do for much of their working lives. Negotiation has only been in the legal training curriculum for the past few years, so it is mainly the recently qualified who have any training at all in what is a fundamental skill. Negotiation is one of the most complex forms of human interaction there is. We cannot conceive of architects designing buildings, or doctors practising, without years of training. Yet we seem to have this naïve belief that anyone can waltz into a dispute and negotiate a settlement without so much as a day's training in how to do it. All ADR training starts, or should do, with a thorough grounding in negotiation skills.

Law	**ADR**
Knowledge of legal procedure	Understanding of human psychology

Of course these are not mutually exclusive, but lawyers seem to be taught very little, if anything, about what actually makes people tick. It is again left to the magic of experience. The bulk of legal education is conceptual, historical, technical, procedural. But disputes arise almost invariably from problems between people, and it seems odd that those whose job it is to resolve problems are not taught more about the human dimension. It would seem sensible, as with negotiation, to teach would-be lawyers at least something about human behaviour. In contrast, most people who train in ADR seem either already to have some psychology training, or end up studying some psychology as a result.

The Legal Response to ADR

What do lawyers think of ADR? They divide into three groups: one enthusiastic, one ignorant and/or sceptical, one actively hostile.

As I have noted in the previous chapter, legal and commercial ADR is being led by a small number of enthusiastic and entrepreneurial lawyers, and they have in turn enthused others who do not want to become mediators, but who recognize the merits of ADR and encourage their clients to use it. We should salute them: to go down such a radically different route in a conservative profession takes both courage and vision. Among these pioneers, there are a number of lawyer-mediators who have said to me that if they could give up being lawyers and make a living out of mediation, they would do it immediately and without hesitation. It is, they reckon, both more challenging and infinitely more satisfying.

As with any spectrum of opinion, the majority of lawyers are in the middle group, and the ADR organizations are working hard to convert them into – if not enthusiasts – then at least sympathizers perhaps sufficiently intrigued by ADR to use it if an appropriate situation arises. Even so, the vast bulk of lawyers have as yet not been touched by ADR. Their firms may belong to one of the networks, or they may have attended a lecture or seminar in which someone like me was wheeled on to talk about ADR, but that is as far as they have got. They usually know what ADR stands for (Another Dodgy Result, for some; an Alarming Drop in Revenue, for others), and they probably think it is a form of non-binding arbitration – the most usual confusion. They do not know enough about it to recommend it to clients with any confidence, but they know enough to fear that it would result in a quick settlement and a consequent loss of fees.

Then there is the final group of lawyers who are actively hostile to ADR and will do their best to ensure that it either sinks without trace, or that it is absorbed into the legal system in such a way that its main benefits to consumers are diluted. What proportion of lawyers belong to this last camp it is difficult to say: one suspects there are more than openly declare themselves. The hostility to advocates of ADR can be fairly vicious and we have to realize that it does challenge enormous vested interests.

So far I have approached mediation largely from the consumer's point of view: and the point usually neglected is that *lawyers are also consumers of mediation*, for the following excellent reasons.

Although no lawyer likes to admit, too publicly, that there is such a thing as a difficult client or an awkward adversary, the reality is that lawyers are faced every day with clients who do not know what they want; are totally unrealistic; want revenge but not the cost of it; and will make hopeless witnesses. And they are faced with other lawyers who do not provide the right information; never return telephone calls; make preposterous claims; and insist on unrealistic settlement proposals.

Lawyers face people and situations which make their jobs almost impossible. It is very easy to be cynical about lawyers, and imagine they are all fat cats enjoying massive salaries from their penthouse offices. There are some like that; but the vast majority work very hard for a modest living, often undertaking some pieces of work with little hope of any return. The stresses, frustrations and insecurities are immense.

Why should lawyers take ADR seriously? It is no universal panacea, but in the right situation it can offer an alternative to the options currently available:

- if a client is nagging for action, a mediation can be set up in a matter of days (or hours, come to that, if the other side is keen);
- if a client needs to let off steam, but is unlikely to win at trial, mediation can provide a risk-free pressure-release valve;
- if a client knows a friend of a friend who got a fortune for a nearly similar injury ten years ago . . . mediation can give them a more realistic idea of what they can expect now, today, in their case;
- if a client is not sure what they want, mediation can help them discover.

ADR also provides a new range of services to be offered in cases where none of the existing services is quite appropriate, and a fresh challenge for those who have stopped enjoying their work. It may be representing a client in mediation, training as a mediator, or helping to facilitate a complex consensus-building process on a vital local issue. In short, while ADR looks as if it is designed to act as a fast track to redundancy for the legal profession, it has much to offer those who recognize the opportunities it presents.

ADR and Consumers

Who are ADR's consumers and potential consumers? Some of these – disputing neighbours, for example – for the most part do not take their disputes to lawyers. Either a dispute rumbles on and goes nowhere; or there is an explosion and the police become involved. Those who do use mediation to resolve a dispute between them usually find it does at least take the heat out of the situation. Another group of ADR consumers has been serviced for some time: couples who are divorcing. Currently the government has plans to encourage an increasing number of couples to see a mediator during their divorce, so this group of ADR consumers is likely to increase dramatically over the next few years.

The largest body of consumers who will benefit from ADR as they become more aware of it comprises individuals, and organizations, who have claims or disputes involving more than £2–3,000 but less than £20–30,000. Such cases may involve anything from equal opportunities or redundancy problems to disputed household or motor insurance claims. These are the routine disputes which pile up on the desks of insurers, claims adjusters, solicitors and surveyors – each one of vital significance to the individuals; each one just another file for a large company. These cases have another characteristic. Given the costs of litigation, and the cuts in legal aid, for many people there is currently no realistic means by which they can be pursued through the courts.

These are the cases where the advent of ADR can really benefit the consumer, as will a number of the recommendations made by Lord Woolf if they are implemented. For example, he recommends an increase in the small claims jurisdiction, and a new 'fast track' system for dealing with cases where the value does not exceed £10,000, with fixed costs and trials to last no more than three hours. While these are still adversarial remedies and therefore not suitable for every case, they will improve the current situation. The combination of simplifying and streamlining the current system and adding the ADR option should make access to justice very much better for everyone.

ADR's potential consumers are not, however, all individuals. Any organization, public or private, which regularly spends money on litigation, or suffers from internal divisions or disputes with clients or customers, should investigate the potential of ADR to preserve its resources and energies.

Chapter 3

Mediation

Mediation is the principal tool in the ADR toolbox. Familiar from news stories about industrial disputes and international conflict, until now, from the consumer's point of view it has been a rather well-kept secret. This chapter concentrates on mediation for two reasons. First, once you have a sense of what mediation is, the whole logic of ADR becomes much clearer. Second, mediation is the ADR process which is going to be of most interest and most relevance to the vast majority of readers.

Let us begin with a few definitions and resolve from the outset some frequent confusions.

Mediation is a voluntary process during which the parties to a dispute meet separately and together in confidence with an independent third party, who designs and conducts a process which enables them to explore and decide how the conflict between them is to be resolved.

Mediation is often confused with *arbitration,* and some people believe they are mediating when in fact they are merely *negotiating* in a conciliatory manner. So:

Negotiation is a process in which parties to a dispute consult directly with each other about possible means of settling it;

Arbitration is a process in which a neutral third party or panel of neutrals meets with the parties to a dispute, hears presentations and evidence from each side and makes an award or a decision.

The really important difference is between mediation and arbitration, as the following explanation of mediation's basic principles will make clear.

BASIC PRINCIPLES OF MEDIATION

The first rule of mediation is that it should involve as few rules as possible. Mediation, especially mediation designed to do more than simply settle a dispute, functions best when there are the fewest constraints on the parties. In fact, one of the first things you have to do as a mediator is persuade people that they can talk about whatever they want to talk about, and they can choose to agree whatever they can persuade the other side to agree.

This rather laid-back approach to the deeply serious business of disputes is probably what makes many lawyers nervous about mediation, but there is a good reason for it. Mediation is not a legal process, concerned with applying rules and regulations. It is a common sense, practical and deeply human process in which people get together to find their way to a workable solution. Sometimes solutions are not very different from what the people could achieve through negotiations or, eventually, in court. But sometimes, for example, a commercial mediation which begins as an argument about a clause in a contract can end with the parties creating a whole new contract and perhaps a whole new line of mutually profitable business. Now, very few people go to court and come away with *more* than they actually asked for.

So the purpose of this chapter is to provide a general overview of mediation as a *generic* process: a process which could in theory be used to resolve any dispute between any people, regardless of the situation. This is not a standard form or model; rather the general cupboard from which any mediator would select the particular ingredients, the particular techniques to be employed, for a particular mediation. These basic principles form the bedrock of mediation, certainly in the sort of general, everyday cases which ought to be resolved by mediation rather than litigation.

1. Mediation is *voluntary*. People should come to mediation because they want to – not because they have been ordered to. Apart from the evidence that court-ordered mediation is less successful, the fact that mediation is voluntary means the parties are sending a useful message to each other: 'We are prepared to sit down and try to work this out with you.'

2. While the mediation process itself is *non-binding*, the final result has whatever force you choose to give it. Normally a commercial mediation ends with both parties initialling a 'heads of agreement', or a joint memorandum setting out what they have agreed. This forms a contract between them, which means it has some legal force. But the process itself must be non-binding so that people feel free to walk away from it if they do not like where it is going. This is really just a logical extension of the voluntary principle.

3. Mediation uses an *independent 'third party'* who has no stake in the outcome and no power to make decisions. The mediator's concern is with the conduct of the negotiation, not with the issues in dispute.

4. Mediation is *confidential*. It is conducted in private, and the mediator will not divulge what happens nor its outcome to anyone outside the mediation without the agreement of those involved. In addition, private meetings between the mediator and each person separately during the mediation are also confidential.

5. Mediation is *without prejudice*. In other words, people can feel free to say what they like, make whatever offers or demands they like, without fear that this will prejudice later legal proceedings if the case is not settled. A classic example of the value of this is when what one person really wants is an apology – but the other person has been advised by a solicitor that it is the one thing they cannot give. In a mediation people can feel free to apologize without fear of the later consequences: if the mediation fails, that apology will not be dragged up in court and work against them.

On this final point, a general note of caution which it would be irresponsible of me not to include. The use of mediation in legal and commercial cases is so novel that questions around the meaning of terms such as *without prejudice* and *confidentiality* in the context of mediation have not yet been tested in court. The general assumption is that mediation is no different in law to any settlement negotiation: one of the reasons why practising mediators talk about mediation as 'assisted negotiation' rather than as any form of quasi-legal process.

THE MEDIATION PROCESS

What actually happens in mediation? Answer: it depends on the people, the issues, the situation. There is no standard form of mediation because there is no standard dispute. There are vast numbers of disputes every year, of course, and naturally some of them have common factors. Contested insurance claims for flood-damaged carpets, for example, are not going to differ wildly from each other. What makes each such case unique, however, is that it involves different people, and each person has their own individual priorities, needs, aversions, motivations and circumstances.

One of the things which makes mediation special is that it recognizes the individuality of each case. Every mediation is a *designer* mediation. There simply is no cook-book recipe for successful mediation: each one has to be designed around what will help the parties to reach agreement. I am emphasizing this designer element because it would be very easy to slip into believing there is just one model of mediation. It is also to counter the disturbing trend, evident particularly among legally trained mediators, of talking about mediation 'procedure' or mediation 'hearings' as if mediation is a legal process.

The first choice to be faced in any situation is fairly straightforward: should there be a face-to-face meeting between those in dispute? If the answer is 'no', then the mediator is forced, by default, into some kind of shuttle diplomacy, and the choice becomes a matter of medium: through meetings, through telephone calls, through exchanges of documents. If the answer is 'yes', the question is '*how* should they meet?' This is where the expertise of the mediator really comes into its own, because the question of *how* is really the essence of mediation – not only how people should meet, but *how* should every meeting happen, every question be phrased. Knowing the answers to these *how* questions takes what we call *process skills*.

Process skills are what mediators use to do everything from planning the first contacts with the parties, to setting up the actual meetings and then conducting the mediation right through to the point of final agreement. If you want to test whether a would-be mediator knows their stuff, ask them which of their process skills they consider the most important. If the answer is not to the effect that it depends on the individual situation and the people involved, you are probably talking to a mediator who approaches every mediation the same way. If your situation suits their approach, no problem. If it does not, then you may want to think again. Precisely how every mediation begins, continues and ends will depend on the situation.

There are, however, some stages common to most mediations, and eventual agreement will usually depend on the parties working through each of these, and sometimes more than once. I will go through a brief description of each stage you would reasonably expect in a mediation between two people trying to avoid going to court over a commercial dispute, and indicate which later chapter covers it in more detail.

I must emphasize again that I am trying here, and in Part Two, to encompass as much of mediation as I can without being prescriptive – every mediation is different and there is no standard process: clearly mediation of a divorce is going to be vastly different from mediation of a business dispute. In this overview I have concentrated on the earlier stages of mediation, because when they ask for a summary of mediation people are usually most interested to know basic things such as how it starts and who the mediator is.

Stage 1: Preparation (Chapter 6)

Usually people come to mediation because one of those involved has heard of its advantages, or is a member of one of the ADR networks. They will probably get in touch with a mediator or a firm of mediators to ask how to take it further. Whether the initial contact is with a firm's case administrator or an individual mediator, that person's first job is to explore, from their independent position, whether the case is *suitable* for mediation and, if so, whether it is *ready* for mediation. If it is both ready and suitable, the mediator will then offer to contact the other side. Experience suggests that an approach from someone who is independent is more likely to achieve an agreement to try mediation than an approach from one of the parties or their solicitor. Those involved in disputes are naturally suspicious of each other, and the suggestion of mediation is understandably met with caution.

If one side is reluctant to go to mediation for fear of indicating weakness to the other, it can be useful to point out that agreeing to mediate is as often a sign of strength as weakness, in that people usually prefer to explore the scope for compromise from a position of strength. Indeed, reluctance to mediate is just as likely to be perceived as a sign of weakness.

Stage 2: Setting up a Mediation (Chapter 7)

Once both sides have agreed to mediation, they will often be asked to sign a formal 'agreement to mediate' (see Appendix A). This identifies those in dispute and their legal representatives if they have them, and the nature of the dispute. It also sets out the terms and conditions on which the mediation will be conducted, and it will probably specify the mediation fee and how it is to be paid. Not all mediators use agreements to mediate, particularly not in the fields of matrimonial and neighbourhood mediation.

Staying with our commercial mediation, the formal 'agreement to mediate' will also name the mediator. It is vital that everyone has confidence in both the abilities and the impartiality of the mediator. This has led some early users of mediation to specify a particular professional background for the mediator. While this is understandable, it reflects a certain misapprehension of what is involved in mediation: there is often an assumption that the mediator's job is to advise those involved how the dispute should be settled.

The single most important qualification for a mediator is the ability to mediate: this should take priority over everything else. When mediators are competent, their other qualifications are of less importance. Understanding the construction industry may be helpful for a mediator in a construction dispute, but it might well be more important to have a mediator with a quite different background who will bring a fresh eye to the problem. A few years ago there was a proposal by a committee of lawyers that mediators should only be selected from lawyers with at least seven years' experience with 'whatever additional training may be necessary'. One suspects here the questionable assumption that the fact of being a lawyer is in some way an automatic qualification to mediate. The fact is that legal training may provide valuable additional expertise for a mediator but the emphasis here is on the 'additional'.

The fundamental skill is that of *mediation*, not law. The personality, mediation training and intuitive skills of mediators are as important – sometimes much *more* important – than any professional training and experience they happen to have. The ability to put people at ease, to defuse tension, to create an atmosphere of creative problem-solving, are just as important as analytical skills or understanding of the issues.

Stage 3: Opening Moves (Chapter 8)

Mediation does not usually begin with a face-to-face meeting. It begins from the moment of the first conversation of one of the disputants with a mediator or a case administrator. Following that, the mediator may meet with each side individually in advance, or there may be preliminary telephone conversations. Some cases are mediated without the parties ever having to meet.

If they do meet, the mediator begins by welcoming both sides, thanking them for attending, and then reminding them of the basic principles of mediation. If the mediation threatens to be very angry, the mediator may propose some additional ground rules, such as 'only one person is allowed to get angry at a time'. This sounds frivolous, but it can help keep things together, and it may offer people a legitimate opportunity to have a go at each other. Without this venting of frustration it may prove difficult to make progress.

After the mediator has introduced the ground rules and set out the process he or she intends to use, each person is then asked to present their story. This is really the only formal part of the process, and it serves two important functions. First, it enables each side to hear a formal presentation of the other side's point of view. This can be very educational and convey all sorts of useful information which was previously obscured: for example, how strongly the other side feels, which may not have been apparent from correspondence. Second, it establishes what the important issues are for that person.

Stage 4: Putting Your Case (Chapter 9)

This stage may last a few minutes or several hours. It is a time for people to vent their frustrations, to tell the other side what they think of them, explain how upset they are, what the situation has done to them. This is a time for *catharsis*, an ancient Greek word for letting off steam and feeling much better as a result.

The mediator, meanwhile, says very little but listens hard, asking occasional questions, checking that every shadow and nuance of meaning is heard if not accepted, and intervening whenever vehemence might turn to violence.

Stage 5: Exploring the Situation (Chapter 10)

When people have had some opportunity to respond to each other – or sooner if the situation is very polarized and they need a safer environment in which to talk about it – the mediator may meet with each side in private. These meetings enable the mediator to be told in confidence anything which the person does not want others to hear. It also gives the mediator an opportunity to explore underlying aspects of the situation which have perhaps become obscured, and which might be too sensitive to discuss openly.

As importantly, it is in the private meetings that people get to know the mediator, and over a period of time begin to develop some trust and confidence in both the mediator and the process. It is often sadly apparent that many people rarely have the opportunity to talk to a professional listener, and sometimes it is simply this opening up of real communication which lays the foundations for resolving the dispute.

Stage 6: Avoiding Power Struggles (Chapter 11)

After the initial hour or two of threats and posturing, people tend to move away from their opening positions, and focus instead on what they want to achieve in order to satisfy their needs and concerns. Sometimes these may have been obscured, over time, by the accretion of legal arguments and the exchange of point-scoring correspondence. It is not unusual for quite complex cases to boil down to half a dozen straightforward requirements from each side.

As the issues become clearer the mediator begins a process of shuttle diplomacy, testing the wind, searching for areas of common ground and potential mutual gains, carrying proposals for settlement.

Stage 7: Getting Creative (Chapter 12)

Creativity is the first victim of conflict, and often the mediator has to help people develop fresh ideas if common ground and mutually acceptable proposals are to be found. This is a delicate process. The mediator must not become too enmeshed in the issues for fear of being accused of bias but must ask the questions which stimulate fresh thinking; isolate possible ideas; run brain-storming sessions; and generally do anything necessary to maintain the momentum of the process and the climate for settlement.

Stage 8: Crafting Proposals and Breaking Deadlocks (Chapter 13)

Getting fresh ideas on the table is not, in itself, enough to trigger settlement. Those ideas have to be moulded and crafted into shapes and forms which will appeal to the other side. By this stage the mediator is playing Devil's Advocate: asking each side to put itself in the position of the other, assisting them to see the situation from different points of view. Even angry people who care not a jot for their opponent's concerns may realize that the dispute cannot be resolved by one side acting alone. It takes two to tango.

This is where the mediator also acts as an 'agent of reality'. Having established a working relationship with each side, it is possible to ask searching questions about the costs of not settling, or the impact of going to trial and winning – and then being faced with an appeal. By now, people are really trying to squeeze every last drop out of each other. The mediator's job is to keep them at it until finally they come up with a solution or package of solutions which solve the problem.

Stage 9: Making Decisions and Formalizing Agreements (Chapter 14)

The final stage of a mediation is to get what has been agreed into writing. Usually a 'heads of agreement' is drawn up, by lawyers when they are involved, and signed by both sides. This will then be turned into a full and formal agreement. The exact form of the agreement is the concern of those whose dispute the agreement has to resolve, not of the mediator, but most mediators keep a close eye on what is written to ensure it matches what has been agreed.

Then everybody goes home, relaxes, and wonders why more people do not use mediation.

* * *

And that is the mediation process: conducted in plain language, dedicated to realistic and practical solutions, designed to bring people together rather than forcing them apart. Too simple to be credible as a way to satisfy angry and aggrieved people? The next chapter explains why it works in over 90 per cent of commercial cases.

Chapter 4

Why Mediation Works

When I give lectures and workshops on mediation and dispute resolution to people who are unfamiliar with the subject, the first half hour usually goes well. I give an outline of what mediation is, how it relates to the practice of law, and some of its benefits. During the second half hour the expressions begin to change from interest to scepticism, so I stop and ask for comments and questions. There are two points which people always want to make. The first relates to something mentioned in my first chapter: our adversarial culture and the systems it has spawned. People are always anxious to tell me that disputes 'have' to be resolved adversarially. Secondly, they tell me, sometimes rather pityingly as if I had spent the last several decades locked up in a Trappist monastery, that human beings are naturally beastly to each other and it is idealistic nonsense to believe they can be anything but beastly. '*Get real*,' they are too polite to say.

This and the next chapter provide some answers to these two related questions: what can be done about the 'adversarial assumption' – the belief that conflict is both inevitable and inevitably destructive; and how can human beings begin to escape from the behaviour and particularly the power struggles which spring from that defeatist assumption? The answers, moreover, are not the stuff of fantasy, but hard-edged, practical lessons hacked out of experience. Faced with them, most people begin to appreciate that conflict and the assumptions and behaviour which sustain it form a *system*. As with any system, if you change one part of it the rest must change too. So this chapter looks at the logic which underpins the 'alternative' approaches to conflict, and the next tackles the human dimensions.

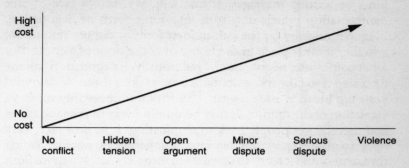

Diagram 1 *The escalating costs of disputing*

THE COSTS OF DISPUTES

Let us begin by thinking about the costs of disputing – and by costs I mean not only the financial ones, but those of time, stress and the strain imposed on individuals and relationships – on an ascending scale. At the bottom is *no dispute* – and *no cost*. Then there is the short, sharp argument, quickly resolved by an apology or a short period of tension. Cost still low – unless it is part of a pattern of conflict which, over a period of time, becomes destructive. Next is the sort of dispute which may land us in the law courts, and that can be anything from the relatively trivial to the very serious. At the top is conflict involving violence, and, ultimately, all-out war: the form of conflict which imposes the highest costs. (And, for the record, I would include both terrorism and prolonged political oppression as forms of war.)

RESPONSES TO DISPUTES

Now let's look at traditional dispute resolution methods. People often try first to ignore a dispute, hoping it will go away. Then, if it cannot be avoided, people try indirect methods, such as dropping hints or writing messages. If that fails, we have a face-to-face confrontation which may turn into some form of negotiation. Negotiation is by far the commonest form of dispute resolution, whether it takes place in the home or at the door of a court. But what comes after negotiation? Traditionally, if negotiation fails the next step is to take more drastic action: make a threat, send round your big brother, issue a writ. This may not necessarily mean an escalation of the dispute. It may be simply a way to raise the stakes and thereby get people back to negotiating. It is, however, very open to misinterpretation because most people do not like feeling threatened, and it tends to drive them into a corner. If negotiations do fail, for whatever reason, then there is recourse to the courts, to arbitration, to physical or economic force and often a combination of these.

Alternative Dispute Resolution expands your range of dispute resolution methods. First of all, it encourages dispute *prevention*. Then it provides a variety of ways to resolve disputes before they escalate beyond the possibility of resolution by negotiation. In fact, it is useful to think of all ADR processes, but mediation in particular, as ways of *extending the negotiating process* – giving people more time and space to sort out the dispute themselves before they have to take it to court or to arbitration and submit their affairs to someone else for judgment. You can think of mediation as extending negotiation in four particular ways.

Extending Negotiations
SOONER
1. Mediation gets people in dispute together sooner by, for example, getting around the old negotiating problem of who makes the first move. The first – transparent – move can be made by the independent mediator.
LONGER
2. Mediation extends the negotiating process beyond the point where normally deadlock might be reached and progress become impossible.

> ### DEEPER
> 3. Mediation extends negotiations by *deepening* the process to bring more understanding of the issues and the differing perceptions of each side.
> ### WIDER
> 4. Mediation encourages the parties to consider the issues in a wider context so that people can focus on common ground as well as on what divides them.

So mediation is not, as people sometimes portray it, an abbreviated or simplified legal process. It is not a legal process at all. It is actually a purely functional means of making a very common process – negotiation – work better.

How, specifically, does mediation improve the process of negotiation? To explain this, we need to look at the four obstacles which often prevent progress in negotiation, and how mediation overcomes them.

Four Obstacles to Successful Negotiation

> **Obstacle 1:**
> *Assumption* that win–lose outcome is inevitable
>
> **Mediation:**
> Starts from the experience that there is always *some* common ground and that a win–win compromise may be possible

People become very nervous around the whole idea of compromise. In our culture, compromise is often perceived to be negative; I have even heard it defined as accepting 'the lowest common denominator'. This tends to ignore the reality that most conflicts do eventually end in compromise unless one side has the power and determination to steamroller all others before it. Besides, it is only the arrogant and the paranoid who refuse to accept that others may see things differently or may have legitimate but different aspirations. All healthy societies rest on the principle that there have to be compromises if people are to live in harmony with each other.

The general principle of compromise does not of course mean accepting compromise in each and every situation. It would not be acceptable, for example, if surgeons mostly remember to sew up their patients after an operation. There are some arenas in which we should strive for perfection 'first time, every time', as the Total Quality Management people like to say. The point here is that, when it comes to resolving disputes within a healthy society, except when it is 100 per cent clear that A is 100 per cent right and B is 100 per cent wrong about everything – which is almost never – the perfect answer is likely to involve a measure of compromise.

Where people go wrong is in assuming, despite this, that compromise has to be negative. It all depends on how the compromise is reached – whether via a process of *win-lose conflict* or a process of *win-win co-operation*. This is because the process of resolving a dispute produces both visible and invisible results. If people start from the adversarial assumption, get into a power struggle, call each other names, and generally try to win at each other's expense, the invisible outcomes (ranging from bad feelings through black eyes to law suits) will tend to detract from the value of whatever they achieve. If they start not from the adversarial assumption, but from a more consensual one, the compromise they reach will bring with it a range of valuable invisible products, such as a working relationship and better understanding of each other's concerns.

It is the mediator's task to help to replace the adversarial assumption and the win-lose process with the assumption that a win-win result is possible, and help people use a process which achieves it. While win-win solutions are not always possible in purely immediate, material terms, the invisible outcomes may more than compensate in other ways. Mediation works because it rapidly becomes clear to people that they may be able to achieve more through working together to resolve a dispute than either could by fighting on alone.

Obstacle 2:	**Mediation:**
Starting from rigid positions which encourage unnecessary secretiveness, deceit and power struggles	Starts from exploration of different and shared needs, interests, fears and concerns

People conventionally negotiate by taking up their respective positions and then trying to nudge towards each other by adopting and relinquishing new positions as they explore each other's flexibility. This process is illustrated in Diagram 2.

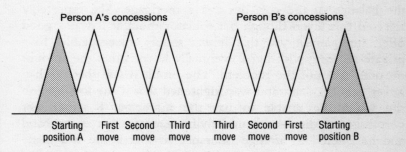

Diagram 2 Negotiating by taking up and relinquishing successive positions

People try to meet each other in the middle by adopting and then conceding a series of positions. This approach works perfectly well in some simple situations, such as negotiating over the purchase of a second-hand car. But it has a number of disadvantages in more complicated situations, and it actually gets in the way when people need to find workable compromises. For example, each move towards the other party depends on the expectation of reciprocal flexibility – that the other side will make a similar move. That in turn increases the incentive for each side to turn the situation into a power struggle. 'Positional' negotiation encourages bluff and counter-bluff, muscle-flexing, playing to the gallery, and all the strutting, posturing and power-playing we regularly see between employers and unions or within the European Union.

It is useful to think of negotiating positions simply as the tips of icebergs on which each side plants its flag and poses for the camera. The position tells you much about people's public ambitions, and what they say from it tells you what they want you to know. For example, a client in a divorce mediation was offered sufficient money towards a house to enable her to fund the balance of the cost through a mortgage. She repeatedly rejected this, even though her solicitor thought it was a good offer: her *position* was that it was simply unacceptable. In a private meeting with her I eventually learned that the amount on offer was not the problem. The problem was that she had never been in debt, and was frightened that if she lost her job she would be unable to pay the mortgage. I gained her permission to discuss this underlying fear with her ex-husband and he offered to arrange insurance so that if she was made redundant the mortgage would be paid. Once this obstacle had been removed, the mediation could proceed.

It is not enough to know someone's position. You need to know: what underlies that position and what do they *really* want to achieve; where the bluff – if it is – ends and the real purpose of their posturing begins; if the positions are incompatible – as they almost certainly are or there would not be a dispute – how they can be moved towards each other. So we have to look below the surface of the iceberg to see what is really going on, what are the interests and values which their positions represent, and, more deeply buried, what are the needs and fears which motivate them. Diagram 3 explains this point further.

When you start digging beneath the surface for interests, values, needs and fears, you begin to discover, as Diagram 4

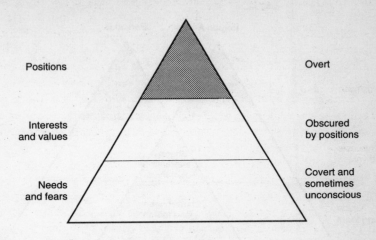

Diagram 3 The PIN (Positions, Interests and Needs) pyramid

indicates, that there are always some which are common to both parties. It is much easier to build agreement *outwards* from the common ground than it is to build it *inwards* from competing positions.

Mediators build relationships with each side so that they can begin to ask sensitive questions about *why* people have taken up their positions, and to clarify what precisely it is they actually want and need. These shared needs and interests form the common ground on which a mutually acceptable resolution of the problem will be built. If you start from shared needs and interests, rather than incompatible positions, then you also set in motion a process which will quickly reveal if there is any measure of agreement on which a larger agreement can be built. More importantly, shifting the focus to needs and interests effectively by-passes the power struggle based on the need to control and dominate the other side by beating down their position.

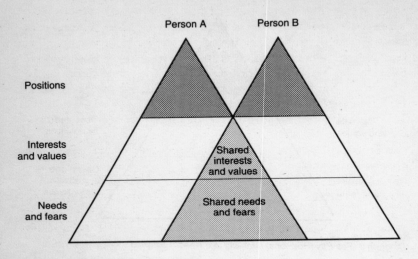

Diagram 4 Mediation starts by looking for common ground

There are one or two more things to be said about this. First, you can usefully think of the difference between positions and needs and interests as the difference between a *map* and the *territory* it represents. The positions are the useful signs and symbols on the map which give you an idea of where you are, but which are incomplete, two-dimensional representations of the real lie of the land. Just as walking your fingers across a map will give you only a partial understanding of the countryside it depicts, so working from people's positions will give you only a partial understanding of what moves and motivates them. If you judge a situation purely by the positional power struggle, you will overlook not only the scope for resolving the situation, but also the scope for a different relationship.

Second, there is another crucial difference between interests and needs. Interests are always potentially negotiable because they are constantly open to influence from new experience, and they can be achieved and expressed in different ways. Needs and fears are, by definition, not negotiable: they either increase or decrease. If something is negotiable, then it is not a need. If this sounds too radical a difference, it is probably because in the modern world we habitually talk of interests as if they are needs, and because very often our real needs are either so easily met that we do not notice them until they are suddenly absent, or they are suppressed beneath the weight of interests. Conflict tends to bring needs and fears into sharp relief, and they have then to be resolved. One of the unfortunate effects of an adversarial process is to exacerbate fears while doing little to reassure people their needs will be satisfied.

Values, meanwhile, need to be explored very carefully. While they are not in themselves negotiable, they usually come in combinations, and sometimes the *relative priority* of values can change if the person who holds them is given sufficient evidence or reasons that it should change. For example, while someone may place a high value on clearing their name in a libel trial, if it seems likely that they will lose, they may put an even higher value on preserving their family's welfare than salvaging their personal pride. Also a revelation to me has been the extent to which even sworn enemies may share some values, and these values can provide a slender basis for starting to talk. Even dealing with environmental disputes where, for example, business people and green campaigners often seem about as far apart as people can be, when you dig and prod and explore in the right kind of gathering, some shared values will always emerge and provide a basis for further dialogue.

Obstacle 3: Adversarial assumptions foster *uncertainties*, and these cause *fear* and *hostility*	**Mediation:** Sets out to reduce uncertainties

Uncertainty is always a key element in any disputed situation, and the shared management and ultimately resolution of uncertainty is a key step towards resolving conflict. After all, if everything is clear and certain, if there are no assumptions to be made, no risks to be run, if people can weigh every factor in the knowledge that they know all there is to know, and therefore it is obvious what decisions are open to them, then really there is much less room for conflict. An adversarial process, meanwhile, exacerbates the problems posed by uncertainty. It makes people hide their cards close to their chests; it encourages them to lie and bluff; it increases the paralysing insecurity of the win-lose assumption; it rewards rigidity and penalises flexibility.

Uncertainties come in three types:

1. There is uncertainty about the *situation*. People usually respond to this by asking for *more information*.
2. There can be uncertainty about what *values* are involved for whom, and therefore the scope for negotiation. People usually respond to this by seeking *outside advice,* more information about the people concerned, or *clarifying the objectives* of each side.
3. There is often uncertainty about *related decisions*. These may be decisions to be made later, or by others, which would affect the situation. This is responded to frequently by the cry for *better co-ordination,* and requests for *delay*.

Very often the hostility in a situation is generated by these uncertainties, since hostility is often the product of fear, and fear is often the product of uncertainty. One of the earliest ways of breaking this destructive cycle and establishing some degree of common ground, even in a polarized situation, is to explore the shared risks and uncertainties and how they might be reduced. Working together to reduce uncertainties is also a potent means of reducing the fears and hostilities spawned by them. So mediators help people to make joint assessments of the uncertainties they face and the risks and consequences if they calculate wrongly. Private meetings with the mediator also mean that people can share their concerns without having to reveal their fears or weaknesses in public.

Often mediators discover that everybody has the same fears: nobody can be quite sure what will happen in the future, or how a third party such as a judge or arbitrator may react. Once the mediator knows about common concerns around risk and uncertainty, he or she can help people to explore various strategies and safety nets to protect their interests, and from these a wider resolution may be built.

Obstacle 4:	Mediation:
Adversarial processes focus on the *past* and *placing blame*	Focuses on the future – restoring relationships and making new opportunities

Every negotiation and mediation is haunted by the past experience of those involved, especially if they have had previous dealings with their adversaries. Even if they have no previous acquaintance with them, there will be echoes of previous situations, past grievances which may not be relevant to the present situation, but which still rankle. Each side will have different expectations based on past assumptions; previous cultural or organizational experiences to draw on; prejudices based on dealing with similar people or situations – sometimes years before. If it is a legal dispute, the focus of both sides will be very much on the past: what has gone wrong, whose fault it was, who should pay how much by way of damages.

Of course the past is important: it influences all of us to become what we are, and it is difficult to understand any situation until we have an understanding of how it has got to what it is. But to concentrate one's focus on the past is not always the most useful way to approach a negotiation which is trying to solve a problem. Revisiting the past can turn into endless attempts to pin the blame or allot the fault exclusively to one side or the other. The key question, at some stage, is: '*What do we do now?*'

The contrast between the law's tendency to focus on the past and mediation's focus on the future is captured in a mediation tool which is sometimes known as the *Blame Frame/Aim Frame*. Like many of the tools used by mediators, such a way to 'reframe' a problem is deceptively simple. People in conflict, particularly those who feel disempowered, tend to think in terms of what they *cannot* do. A re-orientation towards what they *can* do to change the situation will often reveal previously disguised options, and also make people feel more resourceful. It can also provide a useful alternative simply to asking a stream of questions about the future, when a person is still firmly stuck in the past. Perhaps some of the strength of this reframing method lies not so much in the fact of it, but in the follow-through: the questions which follow on from the initial reframe. As you can see, these are not only future-oriented, they contain pre-suppositions that the situation can be changed, and changed by that person.

Blame Frame/Aim Frame

Blame frame:
1. What's the problem?
2. Why has it arisen?
3. Whose fault is it?
4. Why hasn't it been solved?
5. What have you tried?
6. Why didn't it work?
7. What will you try next?

Aim frame:
1. What do you really want?
2. How will you know when you have it?
3. Where are you now in relation to it?
4. What resources do you already have which will help you achieve this aim?
5. What options are open to you — and acceptable to others?
6. Which option is going to get you what you really want?
7. What do you have to do to achieve it — and help others to help you achieve it?
8. What is your next step?

Several years into a dispute, most people are delighted for the focus to be moved off the past, and on to the future, and mediators have the freedom to help them do this. Of course, there is no reason why they should not do it themselves, or why their lawyers should not do it with them. In fact, they probably do exactly this — but not when they are with the people they perceive to be their adversaries. This is because the lawyers, to do their job, must be concerned with 'winning' in terms of the blame frame, and their clients are probably too anxious to risk the uncharted waters of the future. But the mediator's job is exactly this: to help them look into the future so that they may no longer be trapped by the past.

★ ★ ★

The identification of these four particular obstacles to making progress in a dispute, and mediation's clear response to each, do much to explain the growing confidence with which people are beginning to use mediation. This confidence also, of course, contributes to the success of mediation in the same way as the adversarial assumption contributes to the failure of negotiation.

Responding to these 'systemic' weaknesses of the adversarial approach, however, is not enough. The other reason for people's scepticism, with which I began this chapter, is the belief that even if mediation works in theory, human nature will make it useless in practice. The next chapter sets out how mediation can also change the way individual people behave in conflict situations.

First Dimension: Context
Every conflict occurs in a specific human context: home, work, public sector, voluntary sector etc. Conflict often springs from different *assumptions* about what − behaviour, values, approaches − is appropriate or not appropriate in the context.

When the mediator exposes these *assumptions*, much of the conflict is seen to be based on different perceptions of the context. Context-related conflict can be relatively easy to resolve *provided* people can be flexible in their understanding and interpretation of what is appropriate to the context. For example, think of a dispute around the appropriate clothing to wear to work, such as the one a few years ago as to whether Sikhs should be allowed to wear their turbans instead of crash-helmets when riding motor bikes.

Second Dimension: Behaviour and Culture
This dimension concerns what people are doing or saying − how they are behaving. Conflict at this level may be direct and obvious, or it may be puzzling if it is the result of unrecognized cultural, linguistic or non-verbal differences.

Conflict rooted in behavioural differences requires an alert mediator with good powers of observation and sensitivity to the nuances of tone and body language. Private meetings with each person will often help them and the mediator to identify what behaviour is causing the problem, and a strategy for dealing with it. An example of this for me was discovering that the black kids I was working with were failing interviews because, out of respect for personnel officers, they did not look them in the eye. The personnel officers perceived this as 'shifty'.

The advent of 'political correctness' has focused attention sharply on behaviour, and particularly on the dangers of making judgments about behaviour without taking account of cultural differences (understanding *cultural differences* as clumsy shorthand to include differences rooted in gender, race, and class). The value of political correctness in making people think more carefully about what they say and do, however, is unfortunately offset by its tendency to censor and inhibit.

Third Dimension: Possibility and Expectation

This is a more complicated dimension. It concerns people's perceptions of what is possible for them, and what they can reasonably expect. This dimension of conflict often has an irritating, unsettling element to it, resulting from people's realizations that others have different ways of operating and different expectations.

It can be frustrating and exasperating: like the exasperation with which the practical person regards the impractical. A mediator can help untangle it by enabling people to explain what they perceive to be the limitations on what they can do to solve a problem. Conflict at this level can sometimes be resolved when people pool their different resources to solve a common problem, or sit down to explore their different expectations of a project before embarking on it.

Fourth Dimension: Beliefs and Values

People's internal, personal, political, religious or cultural values often shape what they perceive to be 'true' in any situation, and explain why they do what they do.

This dimension of conflict is often vicious because it threatens to undermine people's basic understanding of who they are and how the world is. Belief and value disputes are hard to resolve because they stem from people living by different internal maps of the world. We see the world not as it is – *but as we are*. The mediator can help people first by encouraging them to discuss what meaning a situation has for them – how and why it concerns them, what beliefs and values are involved for them, where it fits on their internal map; and second by exploring how the map may be expanded to include other, different maps. This is probably the most time-consuming aspect of mediation.

> **Fifth Dimension: Identity**
> Conflict nearly always threatens people's personal or communal sense of their own significance – their sense of who they are.

This sense of identity can be composed of all sorts of things: ethnic or cultural origins, social or political allegiances, family background, education and training. It is often unconscious; sometimes its outward expression is limited to symbolic forms, such as flags, rituals, or even clothes – such as those worn by different professions or street gangs. Conflict around this is uncompromising because, whether it is between individuals or nations, it is about physical and psychological survival. The mediator's role is to make sure each side appreciates just what is involved for the other. The ethnic conflicts which are so much a feature of the contemporary world have erupted because old constraints on identity and autonomy – such as those imposed by the old Soviet Union – are no more.

> **Sixth Dimension: Meaning**
> Some conflicts have a meaning beyond the immediate for those involved: people talk, for example, about being involved in something 'bigger than themselves', or have a sense of belonging to a community or movement from which they derive a sense of meaning and purpose for their lives.

This dimension can be hardest of all to grasp if you have no experience of it, but for those for whom it is significant it is very significant indeed because it underpins everything else. One familiar example is the militant environmentalist whose commitment to the cause calls for extreme measures against those who do not share it. This dimension of conflict may also be fuelled by a person's sense of connection with something greater than themselves; in the environmentalist's case, this would be the natural world, perhaps articulated in some symbolic, religious or mystical form. Religious fundamentalism also comes in here.

Conflict which has this dimension is very difficult indeed to resolve. The mediator's role may be limited to helping those who do not perceive or understand this dimension to begin to empathize with those who do.

Finally, it is worth adding that the 'higher' up the dimensions you go (i. e. from context towards identity and meaning) the more deeply rooted the issues become, and the more valuable it is to use a mediator who can interpret each side to the other.

THE IMPACT OF CONFLICT

The next aspect of the human dimension to consider is how conflict affects people, how it affects their behaviour, how it gets in the way of reaching agreement, and what the mediator can do about it.

First Impact: Fear

Our culture – paradoxically, given our penchant for adversarial thinking – sees conflict as 'wrong'. This creates fear of conflict itself, undermines the belief that resolution is possible, and consequently encourages the attitudes and behaviour which make it harder to find common ground.

Conflict is so daunting that we prefer not to think about it too much. It is no wonder that few people, either at home, at school, or in the course of their adult lives, are taught how to handle disputes. This is quite curious, when you come to think about it. After all, disagreeing with others is part of everyday life. If we have time to teach children table manners, or mathematics, or football, you would think we might teach them how to handle the basic situations which all human beings experience.

One of mediation's first tasks is to help people feel safe about dealing with difficult issues by creating a positive, forward-looking climate in which people feel progress is possible.

> ## Second Impact: Communication Breakdown
> Communication is the first casualty in most disputes. People stop listening and start shouting; they put their energy into working out how to get the upper hand.

When they do listen, they tend not to hear what their opponent is saying, but what they think they are saying, or what – given the situation – they expect them to say. And that – rather than what the other person has actually said – tends to be what they respond to. This creates an escalating spiral of poor communication and inadequate understanding. Before long, it becomes impossible for either side to hear the other and communication turns into a morass of misunderstandings, assumptions, prejudices and mutual suspicion.

Mediation makes effective, multi-dimensional communication a priority. First of all, mediators listen carefully to each side in order to assess how the situation is understood from the different points of view. This also gives each side the satisfaction of knowing they have been heard and understood. This alone often helps defuse the situation. When the mediator thoroughly understands the various arguments, he or she will help each side to express their points of view as clearly as possible, and to explain why they feel the way they do. If at any point it becomes evident that something is not being understood the way it is meant, the mediator intervenes and asks for the point to be clarified. Gradually each side comes to understand the other better, and while they may still disagree vehemently with what they hear, at least they are hearing it. Communication is restored and there is some chance of mutual understanding.

> ## Third Impact: Confusion
> Because people are frightened by conflict, they tend to focus on what *they* think are the 'real' issues, and discount the problems and perceptions of others.

This creates a cycle of misunderstanding, and it is not unusual for mediators to discover that people are talking 'at cross purposes'. Sometimes it even becomes apparent that each side has quite a different idea of the issue in dispute.

The mediator helps everyone to agree what the problem is: or to agree a range of issues which need to be discussed, embracing what each perceives to be the 'real' issues. Once each side knows that 'their' issue is firmly on the agenda, they are then more willing to listen to the issues raised by others. Often more issues surface during the process, and the mediator can ensure they are also given proper consideration.

Fourth Impact: Projection

People in dispute tend to see their own behaviour in others — sometimes because they are divided about their own role or interests in the situation.

This is a less straightforward aspect of the human dimension. There is a school of thought which says that all conflict is the external projection of internal conflict: that people become involved in external disputes because they do not want to face up to their internal ones. Unfortunately, involvement in external conflict can easily exacerbate people's internal divisions: it highlights the fractures. The same is true of departments, organizations, and governments: when the going gets tough, the cracks emerge. Paradoxically, of course, this is why conflict can be such a positive and useful experience for an organization, just as it can contribute to the growth and sense of integrity of an individual.

This is one example of how apparently destructive behaviour may at some level have a positive intent. The job of the mediator may be to discover that intent, and help the person find ways of satisfying it which will be acceptable to the other people involved. Where there is cultural or gender conflict, the projections may become very complex indeed, and mediation may dip into psychotherapy before it can make any progress.

Fifth Impact: Disintegration

In an adversarial context, people cannot afford to be less than single-minded about anything, and especially not as far as 'winning' is concerned. And yet people are rarely totally single-minded.

'Part of me wants to fight this all the way; and part of me just wants to settle the whole matter and get on with my life.' In most conflicts people are less than single-minded. They are plagued with fears and doubts, part of them wanting to fight and win, part wanting to duck combat and go for a more peaceful life. The more people there are involved in the situation, obviously the more such 'parts' there are with each person probably wanting quite different things even though on the same 'side'. Very often the mediator will have to help these internal warring 'parts' agree before tackling the actual differences with the other side.

Mediation should help people to explore these internal as well as external divisions. If a mediator suspects someone is unsure about what to do, he or she can, in a private session, help that person to articulate the choices open to them, and clarify the costs and consequences of each. This means that if that individual decides, for example, that the risks and stresses involved in fighting a legal action are not for them, the mediator is available and has the skills to help them design a more co-operative approach. Furthermore, the mediator can approach the other side on their behalf, so they can conduct the negotiation at arm's length.

Sixth Impact: Falling Prey to the Past

Every dispute is haunted by the past experience of those involved, especially if they have had previous dealings with their adversaries.

If it is a legal dispute, the focus of both sides will be very much on the past: what has gone wrong, whose fault it was, who should pay how much by way of damages. Focusing on the past is not just the systemic problem discussed in the last chapter: it shapes the way people feel about the present, their behaviour in it, and their attitude to the other side. Even if they have no previous acquaintance with the actual people (for example, a mediation with an insurance company), there will be echoes of previous situations, past grievances which may not be relevant to the present situation, but which still rankle. Each side will have different expectations based on past assumptions, previous cultural or organizational experiences, prejudices based on dealing with similar people or situations – sometimes years before.

Mediation encourages understanding of the feelings resulting from past experience, but helps people to focus on how they want to feel in the future and face up to the key question: 'What do we do now?'

Seventh Impact: Feeling Victimized
Conflict induces feeling feelings of powerlessness which lead people to overlook the resources they do have.

Power is a factor in every situation, and people often start from the assumption that the presence or absence of it will be the deciding factor in who 'wins' at the end of the dispute. Sometimes they are right, because in an adversarial forum, the most powerful party is often guaranteed to win – even if the price is high and the ultimate result is disastrous for everyone including the 'winner'. The classic example is the person who wins an expensive legal action only to discover the other side has been bankrupted by the legal process.

Different people make different estimations of their power relative to that of the other side: some become over-confident, others freeze. Either response is unhelpful to achieving equitable and sustainable solutions, so mediation attempts to moderate the impact of power as a decisive factor. The mediator's job is to help the parties get what they want. Even if one side holds all the cards: lots of money, plenty of allies, and all the legal arguments are in their favour, it does not necessarily follow the best solution is one which pulverizes the opposition.

If, for example, the dispute involves a planning dispute between a business and a community group, it could be that if the business uses its power to 'win', it will alienate all the people it wants as its future customers. In such a situation it is the mediator's task to ensure that the power differences do not obscure the issues, or spoil the chances of finding a solution which genuinely meets the needs and concerns of all sides. Mediators are therefore trained to use a technique known as 'power-balancing', which simply involves helping each side to appreciate the disadvantages as well as the advantages of whatever power they have.

Power is such an important subject in the context of conflict that it is discussed at some length in chapter 11.

Eighth Impact: Exaggeration of Differences

If you are in dispute with someone it is natural to notice, exaggerate – and resent – the differences between you, be they cultural, social, financial or whatever.

These differences can end up eclipsing the similarities. The current practice of emphasizing the cultural differences of minority groups, for example, may actually make it harder for the majority to accept them because it overshadows our common humanity. It may be wrong: but there is a strong human tendency, certainly at the individual level, to like, admire and respect people who are like us. Building communities means building on common humanities as well as respecting important differences.

Conflict makes it harder to see other people as people just like us, so in the early stages of a mediation, mediators try to help each side recognize that the other does not have horns and a forked tail: that they are human too.

Ninth Impact: Mistrust

Adversarial settings encourage people to be secretive and to mislead the other side, and this limits the chances of developing trust between them.

The first problem with secrecy is that it tends to be indiscriminate, which can deprive everyone of the information they need to reach an agreement. More importantly for the human dimension, it damages the chances of establishing even a working relationship. Without a degree of openness and the feeling of security which that brings, trust remains elusive.

Mediators know that the creation of trust between people in dispute increases dramatically the chances of a good outcome. By acting as an 'honest broker', in private and confidential meetings with each side, the mediator can discuss with each side what it would be useful to reveal, can help them assess the value of secrecy versus the value of reaching agreement, and can help people establish some confidence in the integrity of the other side. The decision whether to reveal information remains, of course, the parties' alone.

MEDIATION'S INVISIBLE BENEFITS

Because some of its major benefits remain invisible, the power of mediation is often underestimated until it has been experienced. It is perhaps these invisible benefits which finally convert people to the principles and practice of ADR, because they are self-evidently 'good'. This is not to say that adversarial processes are 'bad': cross-examination, for example, is sometimes the only way to establish the truth of what happened in a particular situation. But the benefits of adversarial processes tend to be confined to the immediate, and to the single person or party who emerges well.

Even those who emerge from mediation feeling that they did not achieve everything they wanted usually admit that they found the process sensitive to their concerns and helpful in terms of understanding the situation better. Where mediation is successful the invisible benefits combine and prove the advantages of co-operation over competition.

First Invisible Benefit: Mutual Understanding

Working with someone is the best way to understand the pressures and constraints upon them. This does not mean you abandon your own point of view, but it does mean you appreciate better their ways of working, decision-making, negotiation and communication.

Mutual understanding is insufficient, in itself, to guarantee agreement and resolution but without it progress towards them is difficult if not impossible. Even if mediation does not result in agreement, it should at least ensure that people can be content with agreeing to disagree. If the failure of mediation means a continuing legal action, the parties may take some comfort from the fact that they will understand each other's case much more clearly, and this will save them time and money in the preparation for trial.

Second Invisible Benefit: Shared Conceptual Frameworks

Sharing conceptual frameworks is another way of saying 'coming from the same place'. It is particularly important in multi-party situations and those which are particularly complex in human, legal or scientific terms.

The more people and issues there are involved, the harder it becomes for people to communicate successfully. So people try to portray the situation as simpler than it really is, or the concerns of others as less significant than they seem. ('Oh come on, you don't really care about . . . do you?') Unfortunately, simplification has the nasty habit of turning rapidly into over-simplification – which ultimately helps nobody.

A shared conceptual framework means that everybody starts talking about something using the same words with the same meanings, making the same assumptions, applying the same understanding of how the situation has arisen. It is the only way of avoiding the typical cases of poor communication and everyone talking at cross purposes you see on popular television 'discussion' programmes. Moreover, shared conceptual frameworks can be used again in the future whenever it is necessary to communicate with the same people. And if resolving the problem means going out to talk to people who did not take part in the original process, the shared conceptual framework provides a useful starting point.

Third Invisible Benefit: Pooled Knowledge

Everyone carries an amazing amount of knowledge in their head. But everyone's knowledge is different – based on their personal experience, their education, their professional training, their individual insights.

Only by working together can this wide range of knowledge be combined, and information from different organizations, different disciplines, different professions and different cultures be brought together in the same place, at the same time, to form the best possible knowledge base for good decision-making.

This contrasts with adversarial processes which may rest on decrying the knowledge of others, or denying the validity of their experience or insights. More than this, the process of pooling knowledge builds respect for others, even for others with whom one disagrees. By the time people have mutual understanding, shared conceptual frameworks and pooled knowledge, the reasons for working together tend to outweigh the reasons for staying apart. This results in the next invisible benefit.

Fourth Invisible Benefit: the Experience of Collaboration

As people who are lucky enough to work in good teams know, people working together are more likely to achieve a result which is better than they could have achieved by working apart.

This is even more true when it involves bringing together people who can make contributions which are 'hard' (such as knowledge, calculation, certainty and objectivity) with those whose concerns are 'soft' (such as understanding, intuition, ambivalence and subjectivity). The total result of combining these hard and soft elements is what we call 'synergy': the whole becomes greater than the sum of the parts, and this in turn produces the final invisible benefit.

Fifth Invisible Benefit: Commitment

One of the most gratifying aspects of mediation is that mediated agreements hardly ever fail to be implemented. The process from understanding to synergy builds commitment to implementation.

For any decision to be implemented effectively, those who have to do the work need to feel they have been involved in the making of the decision: that they share some 'ownership' of it. This is particularly important in a multi-party situation or where there is a hierarchy involved and the people who make the decisions may not be the same people who have to carry them out.

Commitment also leads to better co-ordination. If people work together in the making of the decision in the first place, they will be more committed to it and less likely to decide something which will not work in practice because they do not know how to work together.

*   *   *

These last three chapters have tried to explain why it is that mediators have such faith in their ability to resolve disputes, and how combining the systemic benefits of mediation with its sensitivity to human needs and diversities, and the invisible benefits that produces, gives mediation a massive advantage over an adversarial process. Part Two will now review the full process of mediation stage by stage.

PART TWO:

Making the Most of Mediation

Chapter 6

Stage 1: Preparation

You are involved in a dispute. Someone suggests mediation. How do you know if it is a good idea?

One of the major delays in the take-up of mediation to resolve legal and commercial disputes is that many lawyers, accountants and other professionals are still unwilling or unable to discuss mediation with their clients. Part of the remedy has been for the main suppliers of mediation to visit law firms and review the use of mediation in specific cases. These visits are offered free to lawyers as part of a mediation service, and to encourage use of it.

CASE ASSESSMENT

This can produce some unwelcome (from the mediator's point of view) results. The most irritating is that the mediator doing the assessment asks exactly the sort of questions which would be asked during a mediation to encourage settlement. The lawyer, recognizing the value of the mediator's distinctive approach, then asks the same questions and settles the case without further difficulty. Marginally less irritating is discovering that the case is completely unsuitable for litigation as well as mediation because one of the parties will choose bankruptcy if it is pursued at all.

Assessing a case as suitable for mediation is only part of the battle. Lawyers feel very possessive about 'their' cases. After all, litigation is one of the main ways they earn their living and justify their existence to their partners. As one outraged lawyer said to me when I remarked that a certain client's circumstances might favour mediation rather than litigation: '*What's it got to do with him?*'

WHEN TO USE MEDIATION

First of all, remember that preventing disputes arising in the first place can be cheaper than even the most sensible ways of resolving them. In any situation where tension is rising and ordinary face-to-face communication or negotiation is not working, calling in a mediator immediately may well save you time, money and trouble in a few months' time when the situation explodes. Equally, if you are going into a partnership with someone, or even entering into a contract, a mediation clause in whatever agreement you sign will make it easier for people to agree to mediation of a problem should the need arise. (See Appendix B for a sample mediation clause.)

Mediation is coming to be used in every type of dispute, from bad debts to whether your aged aunt should be allowed alcohol in her nursing home: there is literally no field of human conflict in which someone, somewhere, is not using mediation. If you find this hard to believe, take a trip to one of the annual conferences run by the Washington-based Society of Professionals in Dispute Resolution. It is truly astonishing. In the United Kingdom we have so far been less adventurous, though you will find a reasonable diversity of cases described in chapter 15. The majority of British mediation cases reported to date have involved insurance claims, construction industry disputes, partnership disputes, and the sort of disputes which arise in the general run of business: contract failures, missed delivery dates, faulty products, disappointed customers, suppliers and contractors.

The suitability of a case is determined not by the type or the subject matter, but by the circumstances of the individual case. Trying to mediate an unsuitable case is a waste of everyone's time and money, which is why mediation suppliers invest time in assessing cases. The following criteria will give you a first impression of whether the particular case you have is suitable. If it meets the criteria below, your next stop should be an experienced mediator or case assessor.

CASE SUITABILITY

The *green* light for mediation:
- You want the case to be settled, and preferably sooner rather than later;
- There are relationships involved which you would like to preserve if possible;

- You want to retain control of the outcome rather than have to accept a judge's or arbitrator's ruling;
- You have a good case, and so does the other side. If judgment goes against them, they might appeal and win. Even if they appeal and lose, the case will absorb yet more of your time and energy before it is finally resolved;
- You are reluctant to spend any further time or money on litigation, but your case has to be resolved;
- There are complex technical issues involved and no guarantee that a judge or arbitrator will fully understand them (a mediator may not either — but a mediator is not going to pass judgment on the case);
- You would like to avoid a trial which might create an unwelcome precedent;
- The situation needs to be resolved by actions which a court cannot order, such as a complicated structured settlement, the re-organization of a company, or the restoration of relationships within a community;
- Your dispute involues someone or a company operating in a different jurisdiction;
- There is a danger that the legal or technical complexities of the case are such that they will overtake the economic and commercial realities;
- A commercial problem has been turned into a legal battle and needs to be turned back into, and resolved as, a commercial problem;
- Aspects of the case could be embarrassing for you if they became public. Mediation offers the opportunity to resolve the matter in private;
- You feel that if some misunderstandings can be cleared up the case may, with a modicum of good will and common sense, be amicably resolved.

The *amber* light for mediation, with caution:

- While the case seems generally suitable for mediation according to one or more of the criteria above, you feel the other side is in a much stronger position, and you might benefit from the protection offered by a formal legal process, (though that of course is no guarantee that you will get it);

- There is a possibility that the mediation will be abused – used just to delay litigation or to gather information. Mediators describe these as 'fishing expeditions' and strongly discourage them: they risk bringing the whole idea of mediation into disrepute.

- **The *red* light comes on firmly in a few situations:**

- You are about to reach agreement anyway and mediation is unnecessary;
- The jurisdiction or sanction of a court is essential for an injunction or to set a precedent;
- There is no motivation for you or the other side to settle short of trial; perhaps because you want to fight, or you are seeking public vindication, or you are just too angry even to meet (in which case a modified mediation process, using first some 'shuttle diplomacy', might be attempted);
- A fundamental point of rights or principle is involved, and it needs to be proclaimed with the full majesty of the law.

There is considerable debate about using mediation in a situation where there has been a history of violence. The more cautious argue that here the court offers some protection. Braver and more radical mediators say that when there has been violence it is essential that mediation takes place as the only hope of transforming the relationships involved. I go for the cautious approach: if in doubt, don't mediate.

Given that the vast majority of disputes are eventually settled out of court, by negotiation, one can argue that a similar majority are suitable for mediation if those involved want to save the time and money used preparing for an event which frequently never happens.

THE 'RIPENESS' OF A CASE FOR MEDIATION

The next aspect of assessing a case is trickier: *when* is it suitable to send to mediation? This, more than ever, depends on the case and the personalities and circumstances involved. Generally there are four 'windows of opportunity' in a dispute:

- The first window opens along with the dispute, at the same time as you are getting or thinking about getting legal advice, and before the dispute escalates. The ADR Group cites this also as the best moment for a 'Pre-Litigation Review' (PLR) meeting, 'at which the parties come together to decide whether they really need or want to litigate, and what information they need to make an informed decision';
- The second window opens after legal proceedings have begun, and a writ has been delivered, because until then the dispute may not be recognized as sufficiently serious to merit any action;
- The third window is after the expense of discovery when you have done enough preparation to have a clear idea of the situation, but you have yet to invest so much in litigation that the only way to recover it is to invest more and more;
- The final window is when the case is more or less ready for trial, and either your counsel has just been briefed or is about to be briefed, and the heavy costs of trial are beginning to concentrate reluctant minds.

Mediation tends to be most proposed during the third window, though as it becomes increasingly used it will probably be employed earlier and earlier and thereby more costs will be saved. There is no reason not to propose mediation at any stage, or not to re-propose it later when the costs and risks have cranked up another notch. Lawyers frequently comment that to propose mediation could be construed as a sign of weakness in their client's case, and this is probably one reason why more cases do not go to mediation. It is the same reason people sometimes leave negotiation too late: fear of being penalized for making the first move.

The same people will often argue, in my experience, that one should only negotiate from a position of strength, which presumably means they are willing to make the first move when they feel strong enough. In reality someone always has to make the first move, whether towards mediation or negotiation. Ideally it should be made on the merits of the case for settlement rather than as a part of some obscure strategy of bluff and double-bluff.

Perhaps in future *refusing* mediation may be construed as a sign of weakness.

Mediation offers a partial way around the problem of who makes the first move. The mediator does it. For some reason this does not seem to be perceived as a sign of weakness, although it may be received, at this stage in mediation's development, with suspicion and scepticism. It is then up to the mediator to explain what is involved.

GENERAL PREPARATION

'To fail to prepare', they say, 'is to prepare to fail.' Nowhere is this more true than in mediation. The overwhelming reason that mediations fail (remembering that, in the legal and commercial arena at least, over 90 per cent are successful) is lack of preparation. There are three types of preparation you need to do: *conceptual*; *emotional*; and *practical*. Ideally every person to be present in a mediation should do them, but in reality this will sometimes be impractical.

Conceptual Preparation

This simply means that everyone should understand the concept of mediation, and in particular that the mediator is not going to act as a judge or arbitrator. There are one or two other aspects of mediation it is also useful to appreciate beforehand:

- The adversarial assumption is ingrained and mediation involves encouraging a fresh 'mind-set' – new attitudes and approaches to a problem. Go into your mediation thinking: '*Let us invest time and effort in the possibility of agreement before we devote our energies and resources to disagreement.*' (Note the *us*.) See if you can get the other side to adopt a similar attitude.
- Mediation is not a panacea: sometimes it just will not work. The most useful approach is one of interested detachment: '*If the process gets me what I want – fine. If it does not, I will get the mediator to adapt it until it does. If it still doesn't, I can simply leave.*'
- The thrust of mediation is not towards discovering who is

---

right and who is wrong in any situation, but to *what people want, and how they can get it*. The final result is what counts. This is one of the most important ways in which mediation differs from a legal process.

— Mediation *tends* to revolve around concrete and specific issues rather than legal arguments. The role of legal argument (if the mediation is being used as an alternative to litigation) is to help you assess the likely results should the case ultimately go to trial.

— Do not be too anxious to set conditions before agreeing to mediation. It may deter the other side, inhibit creativity, and it can result in you painting yourself into a corner before the mediation even starts.

Emotional preparation

— Mediation can be an emotionally draining process — even when it is about completely unemotional subjects. Disputes about anything always have an emotional element, and mediation sets out deliberately to create an environment which will enable you to deal with difficult and painful issues if that is required.

— Mediation, at its best, is a creative process. It works best when people come together not just to haggle around a few well-worn issues, but to kick-start their imaginations about what might be possible rather than getting bogged down in what is probably not.

— Mediation means you control your own destiny rather than relying on someone else — such as a judge or an arbitrator — to tell you what to do. For some people this is the hardest part of it, and you need to be emotionally prepared to take this responsibility. The compensation is that after involvement in a successful mediation people often seem to feel a new sense of self-confidence.

Practical Preparation

Practical preparation is essential not only for those in dispute, but for their professional advisers, especially if they have not been through a mediation before. This section is aimed at solicitors and accountants in particular, who do not always appreciate that preparing for mediation is slightly different from preparing for litigation.

Mediation in any context involves a rigorous analysis of the issues and the exchange of settlement offers. Unlike arbitration or a trial, there is no formal presentation of evidence or cross-examination of witnesses, so preparation is less time-consuming and expensive. On the other hand, it means you have to be clear about what you want to achieve in the mediation, the weight to put on arguments the other side may use, and the costs and risks of not reaching a settlement.

This last point is particularly important. Most legal and commercial mediations, and actually most other types of mediation, eventually boil down to the balance of cost and risk. '*Do I accept the offer on the table – or do I walk out and try for more by negotiating further or going to trial? But what happens if I go to court – and lose? What happens if I go to court and win – but the other side appeals?*'

One of the mediator's prime jobs is to help both sides compute the costs and risks of settling or not settling. Yes, they may be lying through their teeth; sure, there is a huge game of bluff and double-bluff going on. But what if the judge believes them? What if the judge got out of bed the wrong side or just happens not to like your face that day? The law, to repeat and repeat, is a lottery: I know of one prominent firm of solicitors which uses mediation because, they say, of the twenty judges who sit in their local court, only half can be relied upon to arrive at a rational judgment in any given case. Such fears and uncertainties about the outcome of a trial are a powerful reason for settling before it, which is why the vast bulk of cases do settle before trial and why mediation, which involves even more careful cost and risk analyses than most negotiations, works so well.

SPECIFIC CASE PREPARATION

If you adhere to the following preparation strategy you will be able to enter any mediation with confidence. For the sake of clarity let us assume here that it is a dispute between two people, which involves a sum of money claimed by you from the other person.

> 1. Know what you really want, and why you want it. It may be the money alone; it may also be an apology, a vindication of your actions, the restoration of a business relationship with the other person.

Work out what each is worth to you. For example, would you be prepared to renounce some of your claim in order to re-establish a valuable relationship? If so, do you need some sort of apology from them before you are prepared to do this? You will find a further discussion of this point in Chapter 8, when we look at Opening Statements in a mediation. For now, work out what you want in general terms.

> 2. Gather all the facts of the case, and write a chronology of the story, summarizing who did what and what happened at each point.

Try to make it as objective as possible: try not to see it only through your own eyes. The more you are able to see it through the eyes of the other side, the better you will be able to anticipate their arguments.

> 3. Assemble any other information which will support your case: medical evidence, expert reports, counsel's opinion.

Make sure you know what witnesses you could call were the case to go to trial. Identify the issues, legal and non-legal, involved in the case. The significance of a legal argument should be assessed according to the significance it would have were the case to go to trial. Assessment of the legal arguments on either side may determine whether people decide to settle or risk a trial of their arguments in court.

> 4. Summarize the strengths and weaknesses of your case on one side of paper. Do the same for the other side's case.

Put the two pieces of paper side by side. To put it crudely, your strengths are their weaknesses, and vice-versa. How best can you exploit your strengths and their weaknesses? How best can you minimize your weaknesses and their strengths?

> 5. When you have done that, you can develop the tough questions you will want the mediator to put to them.

The only power mediators have to help your case is the power you give them. The better prepared you are, the more likely it is that you will be able to get the terms you want.

> 6. Decide what you want to send to the mediator in advance. Some mediators may ask to see the pleadings – each side's formal statement of the case – others prefer nothing at all so that they have no preconceptions about the case.

Regardless of what the mediator asks, you would be well advised to write a brief summary – two pages at most – of the facts and your arguments. It will help to make you articulate and confident in your presentation of the case.

> 7. When you have done all this, you are in a position to consider your tactics during the mediation. First, decide what you want to do with the information and arguments you have gathered.

Information comes in five types:

Information which forms the 'common knowledge' of both sides.
Because information is widely regarded as a source of power, people are often reluctant to share it at all. It can be useful, at an early stage in a mediation, to establish the information which is held in common by both sides. The explicit acknowledgment of

what both sides can be presumed to know is a subtle way of beginning to identify common ground.

Information you are happy to disclose to the mediator and the other side.
If this information is likely to come out during 'discovery' (the compulsory disclosure of information prior to trial), there may not be much to lose by disclosing it during the mediation. Indeed, the more open you are from the outset, the more likely the other side is to relax and be equally open. It is part of the process of building a problem-solving rather than point-scoring relationship.

Information of whose significance you are unsure.
If this is the case, the best advice is to discuss it first with the mediator in confidence. He or she will help you assess the advantages and disadvantages of disclosing it to the other side. If still in doubt, use the precautionary principle: do not do anything which you cannot later reverse.

Information you are prepared to disclose only to the mediator in confidence.
You will probably not want to do this at first – until you have gained some faith in the mediator's competence. When you have, the more information you can give the mediator, the better. Make quite sure the mediator knows what he or she can divulge, and what must not be revealed at any cost.

Information you keep to yourself.
You have an absolute right not to divulge anything nor budge an inch in mediation. If you choose this tactic, however, you risk the other side feeling the whole thing is a waste of time and walking out – which is not helpful if you need a settlement.

As mentioned earlier, there are occasions when people try to use mediation as a 'fishing trip' to see what they can find out about the other side's case without giving anything away. The other side usually discerns this, which can polarize the case still further. Another effect is to annoy the mediator, who is quite likely to stop the mediation on the grounds that you are not participating in good faith.

8. Next, work out how best to use the mediator. The mediator is, at the very least, a channel of communication to the other side.

But a mediator can be much more than this:

- a Devil's Advocate, using your arguments against the other side (and theirs against you);
- a problem-solver, helping you to come up with fresh ideas for breaking a deadlock;
- an 'agent of reality', helping both sides assess what is realistic in the situation.

9. While you are thinking about what information to hold or use, and how to use the mediator, you can begin to make a negotiation plan.

What will be the best way to persuade the other side to give you what you want? What could you offer which would be of more value to them than it is to you? The classic negotiation strategy is always to cede something of little value to you for something of more value. The trick is to appreciate what *you* have which *they* want – and ask a price they will be willing to pay. Always be realistic. Starting with a massively inflated demand may make you feel important, but it probably doesn't fool them and it may just mean making more concessions later. Start with a figure you can justify – and do so. After all, if you cannot justify your own demand, how can you expect them to meet it?

10. As you think through your strategy, begin also to construct your 'opening statement'.

The precise form this should take is discussed in Chapter 8.

> 11. When you have decided on your strategy and your opening statement, you are in a position to decide, if you have others with you, who should do what.

In cases where a client is represented by a solicitor, for example, the client quite often simply sits and listens during the initial sessions, only becoming involved if his or her opinion is needed or an additional point needs to be made. More active participation by the client, however, and especially during private sessions with the mediator, has much to recommend it.

In fact, I believe clients should, wherever possible, be taking the lead role in mediation, and their representatives should be in the supporting role. This is not always practical: an inarticulate client on one side and a loquacious Queen's Counsel on the other is frustrating for both. But if mediation becomes simply another setting in which lawyers try to get the better of each other, then it will be failing. Clients bring to mediation something which their lawyer never has: a personal stake in the outcome.

Whether the running is to be made by client or lawyer or other supporter, plan in advance who will do what at which stage.

> 12. Finally, be clear about your authority to reach agreement.

If you are negotiating on behalf of an insurance company in a claims settlement case, you may have a fixed amount you can offer and no more. Make sure you know what it is and if there are any circumstances in which it can be exceeded. In such situations it is a good idea to establish in advance to whom you can turn for extra authority to settle a case should you need it. Equally, if the agreement of your partner, professional or personal, is essential before you can make a decision about anything, make sure they are at the mediation. If that is impossible, at least make sure they can be reached by telephone throughout the mediation.

GENERAL PREPARATION NOTES

You can consider yourself prepared for any mediation when you can answer confidently the following questions:

1. What *specifically* do you want?
2. How will you know when you have it?
3. What do you want to avoid?
4. Do you want a future relationship with the other side? What is it worth to you? What would be the consequences of losing it?
5. What is the absolute least you need to achieve?
6. What is your Best Alternative To a Negotiated Agreement (BATNA)?
7. What is your Worst Alternative To a Negotiated Agreement (WATNA)? Using the BATNA and the WATNA, what range of agreements would be acceptable to you?
8. What issues, from your point of view, are negotiable? What are not, and why not?
9. Who should be present at the mediation? Who should at least be represented?
10. How many negotiations are there? Are you just negotiating with the other side? Are there negotiations within your own side? Are there negotiations within the other side? How can you influence those negotiations in your favour?
11. How should you communicate what you want? What impression do you want to make on the other side? How much pressure should you apply at the outset? At what stage should you communicate what you really want?
12. What might be the other side's opening move? How should you respond? What should you do if their opening is outrageous?
13. Which of your strengths do you want to exploit? How best can you do this? What effect will it have on the other side?
14. Which of their strengths do you need to neutralize? How can you do this? Could any of their strengths work to your advantage?
15. What weaknesses do you want to hide? How can you do this? If you cannot hide a weakness, how can you at least limit its impact?
16. Which of the other side's weaknesses do you want to exploit? How can you do this? Is there a danger of them

walking out if you do? Will it help to drive them into a corner?

17. Is there any other information you require in advance?
18. What information should you disclose to the other side?
19. What information should you disclose only to the mediator?
20. What general principles (legal, moral, financial) might help you make your case?

★ ★ ★

By the time you and your supporters have worked through these questions once or twice, you will feel well prepared for either negotiation or mediation. Let us say you have one last go at trying to negotiate directly with the other side. It fails, and you decide mediation is your best chance of not seeing them in court. The next chapter takes you through the process of setting up a mediation.

Chapter 7

Stage 2: Setting up a Mediation

You already know that your case is suitable for mediation, your last shot at direct negotiation has not worked, and you have done enough of the preparation work described in the previous chapter to know what you will do if the other side agrees to mediation. You now have to get them to the negotiating table. *The negotiating table.* When you read newspaper or television news reports about wars or industrial disputes or football managers and their clubs falling out, there is always someone saying: *'I hope we can sort it out around the negotiating table.'* There is this cosy belief that if you can just get people around the negotiating table then somehow everything will be fine.

The truth is that getting people to the table is often harder than getting them to agree once they are there. This is certainly the case with mediation in every context in which I have ever worked. Getting people to agree to meet is a long process of coaxing, and reassuring, and nudging them towards making the noises which will encourage others to agree to come.

Let me offer an immediate example. While I was writing that paragraph the fax machine beeped and burped out the concerns of an organization which is shortly due to attend a mediation with one of its public critics. This is January. Mediation was first mooted a year ago and rejected. Last summer the idea was resurrected, and this time there was a tentatively positive response. There followed much shuttling between the two sides. Who should attend? Where should the meeting be held? What should its purpose be? We worked steadily through the autumn, clarifying what might be achieved, discussing the various forms the mediation could take, exploring with both sides what each wanted to avoid.

The first good sign was the agreement, at long distance, of a joint statement to the press to be released should news of the meeting become public. That reflected the fears on both sides that meeting the other would be seen by their respective supporters as a betrayal. Meanwhile, parallel with these clandestine contacts both organizations were laying into each other as usual, proclaiming the impossibility of any relaxation in the state of war between them.

The first meeting is a month away, and both sides are getting jumpy. This afternoon's fax was to ask my advice on the wording of one side's opening statement. It is cautiously positive, forward-looking, emphasizing the need to find common ground if it is possible. The only bit I shall try to change is where they say that they have more in common with their opponents than they have differences. I think that is presumptuous: if I was in their opponent's shoes I would instantly want to prove just how different I was. Will the meeting ever take place? I think the chances are slightly better than even with this one, though I rather doubt it will take place on the day it is scheduled. One side or the other is likely to cancel at short notice, just to show that they do not want to meet that badly. So it goes.

[I was wrong. The meeting did take place after further careful preparation. Although there were some tense moments, on the whole you would never have guessed the long state of open warfare between them. There was even some nervous merriment. At the end they agreed to a further series of three meetings to discuss the major issues between them based on the small measure of common ground established at this first meeting.]

AGREEING TO MEET

Getting people to mediation is an art in itself. There are three things to remember when you are trying to persuade the other side to agree to mediation:

1. The mediation begins as soon as you decide to do it. From that moment on, the prime need is to search for the common ground and the possibility of agreement in *everything* you do. The mediator, once appointed, will help both sides find terms on which you can meet.

What if the other side responds negatively to your proposal of mediation and says it is a lousy idea? You agree and say perhaps it is a long shot, but shall I check it out and let you know what I can find out anyway? Your only aim and purpose at this point is to get them to that table, and everything you do must be devoted to that. If you are afraid of appearing weak, tell them you want mediation because you know you have a good case and you do not want to waste your time and theirs proving it.

2. The other side may not understand the concept of mediation, so when you suggest it, they will be suspicious, and they may assume that you have a tame mediator in mind who will take your side. You need to reassure them that mediators have no power to make decisions so even if they are biased they cannot force anyone to do anything they do not want to.

In legal and commercial cases it is often the mediator or the mediating body's case administrator who approaches the other side on your behalf. This is because they are usually experienced in explaining how mediation works, answering questions and allaying suspicions. If, however, you are on sufficiently good terms with the other side, you can yourself suggest mediation as a mutually acceptable way out of your dispute.

3. Getting people to agree to meet is a negotiation in itself. They may try to get you to make concessions as the price of their attending the mediation. The best advice on this point is to reply that you think the mediation is really the best place to discuss the substantive issues.

If you want to give them some incentive to attend, or do something positive to demonstrate your good faith, invite them to pick times and dates for the mediation. Getting an agreement to meet is most important, at this stage, and if being in command of such details makes them feel good, it is a small price for moving towards agreement on the larger issues.

THE 'AGREEMENT TO MEDIATE'

The final part of preparation for mediation is for the disputants and the mediator to sign an 'agreement to mediate'. This sets out the terms and conditions under which the mediation takes place. It stipulates the confidentiality of the process, the impartiality of the mediator, and the 'without prejudice' nature of mediation. Where appropriate it also says who is paying for the mediation. Normally, and preferably, the mediator's fee is split evenly between the parties, but one party alone may finance the mediation providing the other party agrees. In this case, the mediator can be protected from suspicions of bias by not being told who is paying for the mediation. If the mediator does know, people can be assured that there are two other safeguards for the neutrality of the process: the professionalism of the mediator; and the fact that the mediator cannot in any case impose a decision on the parties.

A formal agreement to mediate tends to be the preserve of legal rather than community or family cases, but there is an argument for advocating it in more situations. It subtly emphasizes that mediation is more than just an ordinary discussion or negotiation and is reassuring for both mediator and clients – everybody knows where they stand. It can also help to set the tone for the occasion, and ensure that both parties recognize the opportunity represented by the mediation. There is an example of a formal agreement to mediate in Appendix A.

CHOOSING A MEDIATOR

What makes a mediator? It is difficult to provide a complete answer because so many different people work as mediators. There are, however, some innate *qualities* which most seem to have in common; certain *skills* which all of them work to acquire; and a range of *techniques*, less personal than skills, which they pick up from experience. Unfortunately, there are not always clear dividing lines between qualities, skills and techniques. *Listening*, for example, has an element of each. Some people are natural listeners: it is one of their qualities, they are skilled at it, and they consciously or unconsciously use certain techniques to make their listening effective.

Rather than being drawn into a debate about what is a quality and what is a skill, it is more useful to focus on what mediators actually have to *do* in order to be effective.

GENERAL MEDIATION SKILLS

1. Listening and Empathizing

> Choose mediators who listen more than they talk.

We live in a time when self-image and self-esteem are considered to be very important. Public success, particularly the sort of success enjoyed by broadcasters, pop stars and politicians, seems to rest as often on self-importance as on genuine merit. This means that our role models for success do not encourage skills, such as listening, which require some degree of self-effacement.

An inflated ego is a powerful barrier to listening properly, and even more to empathy – the ability to step out of one's own shoes and into those of someone else. Mediators not only have to be able to empathize in order to understand the perceptions of others, they also have to help those others – often with powerful egos suffused with rage and self-righteousness – to do likewise. Progress may demand that people begin to appreciate the points of view of those who are very different from themselves: people from a different culture, perhaps, or people who feel they are the powerless victims of the situation.

Listening and empathizing demand similar skills. They both require an investment of time and energy; the ability to ask probing questions gently, reflecting the tone as well as the content of what has been heard. This means being sensitive to what has *not* been said, and especially to the deeper issues and values involved for someone; all the time subtly affirming the right of people to hold their views, and acknowledging the personal significance of the individual's role in the situation.

> Things to look for in good mediators:
> — occasional nods and grunts to show they are listening to you;
> — they seek clarification of what you are saying from time to time;
> — they regularly paraphrase what you have said, playing it back and seeking confirmation that they have heard you accurately.

All the while, the mediator should be aware that this sort of 'active' listening can be intrusive if carried to extremes. There is sometimes a fine line between attention and interrogation.

'Active listening' is also used by mediators to get the speaker to acknowledge the emotional content of what they are saying. So often disputes cannot be resolved until people have released their feelings about a situation. For example, you say: '*He refused to pay me what he owes me.*' The mediator observes signs of your tension and distress, such as a flush on the face or hunched shoulders, and responds by saying something like: '*Did you feel your trust in him had been betrayed?*' or '*You must have been very angry with him.*' This gives you the opportunity to confirm such emotions: '*Yes, I was furious!*', or indicate different ones: '*Not so much betrayed, as frustrated that he valued our relationship so little.*' The mediator can then discuss the next step to be taken.

Training in active listening is essential for mediators, though the use of it continues to be debated because some mediators feel it can 'lead' clients to express emotions they do not really feel. Like all mediation skills it has to be used with care and discretion, and in a way which works for the individual mediator when working with the individual client.

2. Sensitivity and Responsiveness

> Choose a mediator who seems sensitive to you.

A mediator's eyes and ears need to be fine-tuned to the subtleties of language, expressions, postures and perceptions. This sensory acuity is an essential adjunct to listening and empathizing, because people communicate with more than just their words. As numerous books on public speaking will tell you, well over half of the communication between human beings is visual — posture, gesture, expressions — and most of the rest is conveyed in voice tones. The word content of the communication conveys a very small amount of the meaning — usually estimated at under 10 per cent — so letters, as a means of communicating, are less than satisfactory. Any profession which leans heavily on written communication can expect to create misunderstandings.

> Things to look for:
> - close attention to words and meanings;
> - a responsiveness to what you are *not* saying as well as to what you are;
> - self-awareness: saying and doing things with care and deliberation.

3. Questioning

> Choose a mediator who asks questions which are 'open', challenging, yet also sensitive and perceptive.

The 'questioning' skill of a mediator may be difficult for you to test before the actual mediation. Questioning is a basic tool: one could sum up the ultimate skill of the mediator as being able to ask the *right* person the *right* question in the *right* way at the *right* moment. The real skill is, of course, knowing what all these 'rights' are.

Good questioning supports and affirms the participation of the person being asked, challenges them to respond creatively even if the question is difficult, and enables them to 'own' their response even if it is uncomfortable for them. Good questions are usually 'open' and encourage people to think, and to provide information and ideas which move the process forward, as opposed to 'closed' questions which can only be answered with 'yes' or 'no'.

> Look for a mediator who:
> - frames questions in a way and language sensitive to your views, values and education;
> - asks questions which show a grasp of the realities of the situation, and inspire you to make a productive reply;
> - avoids using technical jargon.

4. Ability to Create Trust

> Choose a mediator you instinctively trust.

The ability of a mediator to inspire your confidence and trust is the single most important factor in making your choice. Sometimes this ability seems almost a magical quality, but when you analyse closely what they do, you will probably realize that you trust them because they do all the things mentioned in points 1 to 3. They listen closely, without being judgmental; they are able to empathize with you; and they ask questions which demonstrate real understanding of your predicament and how you are feeling. There are also personal attributes to look for:

> - they are self-confident without being arrogant;
> - they are sensitive without being passive;
> - they can challenge you without being aggressive.

If a mediator cannot win the trust and confidence of those in dispute, none of their other skills can be deployed. Likewise, a mediator may demonstrate all the human skills, all the listening and empathizing, but if you pick up some incongruity between what the mediator says and what he or she does – some fleeting, intuitive feeling of dissonance – then you will rightly withhold your trust. This was brought home to me recently in a training workshop which included a very bright, competent and pleasant professional woman. She was participating as part of a mediation team in an exercise which was being videoed.

The exercise seemed to go well enough at first, but it gradually became apparent that something was not right, and eventually the exercise ended in some disarray. When we went back over the film afterwards, it became apparent that the participants had simply not trusted this woman: it was visible in their body language during her interventions. When we asked why this was so, they said she was not 'walking her talk' – there was some dissonance between what she was doing and what she was saying she was doing, and because of this they felt patronized and unable to trust her. It was a harsh but immensely valuable lesson for her.

5. Ability to Manage the Mediation Process

Choose a mediator who has a natural authority.

Mediation may be less formal than a legal process, but this makes its design and management even more important. A designed mediation heads in a more or less pre-determined direction with a pre-determined purpose, even if its course and final result are unpredictable; if not designed it can easily descend into chaos. One of the reasons most people are sceptical about mediation, and particularly multi-party, consensus-building mediation, is that they are probably used to undesigned meetings. On one occasion one of the participants informed me on his way into a multi-party meeting that it would last an hour at the most, and even then we would be lucky to get out without blood on the carpet. I finally had to end the meeting some six hours later. My sceptical friend was amazed that it was possible for angry people to talk to each other so constructively.

Mediators need an innate authority so that they can establish an arena of trust and mutual respect on all sides. Then progress becomes possible. The ability of the mediator to do this may, again, not be evident until the mediation itself: but if you feel an instinctive respect for your mediator, there is a chance that others will too.

> Once you get into the mediation, the signs of a well-managed and productive process are:
> - People listen to each other;
> - Relationships are stabilized and begin to improve;
> - There is a clear agenda and issues are discussed systematically, purposefully, and in depth;
> - People's differing needs and interests are being acknowledged as legitimate;
> - People are constantly looking for common ground and seeking to reconcile different perspectives.

The general rule is that a good *process* produces good *results*. It does not guarantee them – nothing can – but at least a good process doesn't add any problems, as a poor process will, to the complexity or intractability of the issues.

* * *

From this summary you will appreciate that there is perhaps more to mediation than meets the eye, and as the 'technology' of mediation develops, so our understanding of the skills required increases, and the more rigorous becomes training for mediators. There is a danger, however, in disappearing entirely down the technical route. It must be emphasized that mediation is, when it comes to the crunch, pre-eminently a *human* process – which is why this section began with listening and empathizing as the key skills, and highlights the personal ability to create trust and manage the process with a natural authority rooted in the personality of the mediator.

CHOOSING A VENUE

Venues tend to be selected by the mediating body, which should be familiar with local possibilities. It is important that the place chosen is appropriate to the needs of the meeting – in particular, there must be enough room for those involved to feel comfortable. There is nothing worse than forcing people who dislike each other to be crammed together in too small a room. This is where the mediator has a housekeeping role, but you as a client should have some say.

The nature of the venue chosen will be influenced on two counts by the nature of the mediation. First, the number of different parties will determine the size of meeting room required; second, the nature of the dispute will determine the type of atmosphere you need. If it is a community dispute involving lots of different factions, a good-sized church hall, community centre or even a pub might be suitable. If it is a mediation to resolve a custody dispute between desperately unhappy parents, then only one room may be necessary, and it should be warm and reasonably intimate. If it is a formal mediation to end a long-running legal dispute, then a number of offices or conference rooms in a hotel will make sense. Ideally there should be one large room in which everybody can be seated for joint sessions, and a series of smaller rooms for each party in which private, confidential meetings can be held with the mediator.

CHOOSING THE ROOM LAYOUT AND EQUIPMENT

Setting up the physical arrangements for the mediation tends to fall to the mediator, but as the client you should know what to expect and be ready with suggestions if what is offered does not seem appropriate.

The nature of the occasion should determine the furniture and equipment required. A two-party mediation of a business dispute is normally conducted around a table, probably with the mediator at the head and the clients and their representatives on either side. Alternatively, the mediator may sit the clients on the same side of the table, and sit across the table from them. Family and neighbour mediation may be conducted in easy chairs, with perhaps a low table between the clients and the mediator or mediators placed strategically between them. In such situations the likelihood of intense provocation and even physical violence may have to be taken into account and affect seating arrangements.

A multi-party consensus-building process, on the other hand, is very difficult if you have people sitting around a table, or behind tables in an open square. Those television pictures of diplomats and politicians eye-balling each other across ten feet of mahogany bring tears to the eyes of every mediator. Large tables inhibit personal interaction and encourage the sort of posturing which obstructs effective negotiation. A consensus-building process requires lots of large, blank walls on which sheets of flip-chart paper can be pinned or stuck: make sure this can be done before the room is booked. The tables should be moved so that the chairs can either be arranged in a semi-circle, or in small groups with tables between them or behind them. People may have enough barriers between them already, so avoid these being reflected in the layout of the furniture.

Flip charts are useful in any mediation: they provide a means for the mediator to help people to focus not on each other but on the issues written down. They are also invaluable for recording progress and ideas, especially in brainstorming sessions. Some of the most productive meetings I attend are conducted entirely on the blank flip-chart-papered walls of the meeting room. The agenda is constructed on the wall; information delivered is noted on the walls; and action points go up there too. At the end of the meeting, our facilitator whips out his camera, photographs the walls – and everyone gets photocopies of the flip-chart sheets in the post. Nobody has to take the minutes, and there are no arguments about the accuracy of the record.

Finally, check with the mediator that there will be a telephone available should you need to consult with someone during the mediation, make sure the room is adequately ventilated, there is a good supply of tea, coffee or soft drinks, and there is something to eat if the proceedings are expected to run into a meal time. Mediation can be hungry and thirsty work.

★　★　★

So, you have decided mediation is appropriate to the situation, you have prepared your arguments and your negotiating strategy as carefully as you can, you have selected a mediator in whom you have confidence, you have agreed the terms of his or her appointment, and you have agreed a venue for the mediation and ensured that appropriate equipment and facilities are available should they be needed. It is time to mediate.

Chapter 8

Stage 3: Opening Moves

The time, place and mediator are agreed. The day dawns; you arrive and are greeted by the mediator and introduced to the other side if you have not already met. The atmosphere is slightly strained as you accept a cup of coffee and sneak a look at the opposition.

Their lawyer looks tough! Why have they brought along that funny-looking bloke with the bulging briefcase? Have we got everything we need? Have we got enough? You look for reassurance to your solicitor, who persuaded you that mediation was a good idea. You know the mediator is good: surely she will support your case? Oh, of course mediators don't support either side, do they?

The mediator says it is time to begin and ushers you to a seat. It is a big round table, and the mediator sits between you and the other side, so you are not staring across the table at them, but neither are you quite sitting side by side. There is a stand with a pad of large paper the other side of the table.

The mediator begins to speak:

'*Good morning, and thank you for coming along. My name is Sally . . . and you have asked me to act as your mediator today. I was selected because I have some experience of helping people to find solutions to the sort of problem you have. Before we go any further, I just want to make sure everyone knows who everyone else is.*'

She looks around the table; everyone nods. You note that her tone is quite formal, but also relaxed.

'*Good, thank you. First, there are a couple of points I would like to make about mediation and how we will work today. As I think your advisers will have already explained, mediation is not like going to court, and my job is not to tell you who is right and who is wrong here. My task is to help you work out an agreement which suits you. The fact that you have agreed to mediation is an excellent start. I expect you are feeling somewhat anxious about it though, as I understand none of you have been through a mediation before. Is that right?'*

She smiles as everyone nods again. She sounds cheerful and confident.

'Well, it is not so bad, and it gets easier when you understand mediation and what we will be doing, and what my role is. Mediation is best described as a way to continue negotiation when it has become too hard without some assistance. In a moment I will ask each of you, or your representatives – as you choose – to describe in turn the situation from your different points of view. When you have done that, I may ask you to repeat or clarify anything I have not fully understood, and then we will begin to work towards a solution.

'My job is to help you identify particular issues which need to be discussed, to help you clarify your respective needs and interests, and to keep you focused on possible ways forward.

'As I think you already know, mediation is a voluntary process, and I have no power or authority to impose a decision on you or force you to do anything or accept anything which you do not wish to. It is also "non-binding", which means that if at any time you wish to leave, you may do so and pursue or resume whatever course of action you choose.'

There's part of your answer: she cannot tell you to pay what the other side are asking. But if the mediation is non-binding, and she has no power, how can it settle anything?

'Non-binding refers to the process, not the result. Should you reach an agreement, as I am sure you will, that agreement will have whatever force you choose to give it. Agreements reached in mediation are normally drawn up as contracts between you, and would therefore have some force in law.'

That's all very well, but part of the problem is that they can't be trusted. They could just ignore the new contract and we will be back where we started.

'In fact, we find agreements reached in mediation rarely need enforcement. By the time we have finished you will have discussed the situation so thoroughly, and the risks and costs of agreeing or not agreeing, that you will only reach an agreement if that is genuinely the best way

forward for both of you. If the agreement has to include matters over which you have no control, we can devise a safety net so that everybody knows what is to happen if something goes wrong.

'*My job ends when you reach agreement, though I will help you make sure you draw up an agreement which reflects what you have achieved. I must emphasize, however, that the responsibility for drafting it, and for implementing it, will be yours alone. Are there any questions at this stage?*'

She sits back and looks around the table. You ask her: 'If we do not reach agreement, does that mean the legal action continues?'

'*Yes. Your legal rights are unaffected by the failure of mediation, and it is 'without prejudice' to your case if there is a court hearing later.*

'*Now, my role. It is a general rule of mediation that the mediator helps with the process of reaching an agreement without becoming involved in the substance of that agreement. This means that I am here to help you to negotiate — not to advise you on legal matters or on anything else. That is the job of your professional advisers. If I were to start offering my advice I would hardly be staying neutral.*

'*I will say a bit more about my independence and neutrality. As I have already affirmed to both of you, I have no previous knowledge of either of you, or of this case. Should I discover in the course of the mediation that I do have some connection with it, then I will say so and I will withdraw from the case immediately if either of you thinks it could affect my role. Otherwise, I will only terminate the mediation if it is clearly not going to succeed, or if I feel that one of you is not participating in good faith: which I am sure is not the case.*'

She may be sure of that: you certainly aren't and you certainly don't trust that other lot. If what she says is right, though, there is no harm in giving them the benefit of the doubt. If it doesn't work you'll have them in court before they can blink. Well, it may take a couple of years . . .

'*You will also be pleased to know that this process is completely confidential, and that I will not divulge what I hear in the course of it. This confidentiality will be maintained should the mediation fail, so you will not be able to call me as a witness if there is ultimately a court hearing.*

'*The next point I wish to make is also regarding confidentiality. When you have each made your opening statements, I will probably ask to speak with each of you separately. These private meetings are confidential: they give us the chance to talk about aspects of the case which you may not want to discuss openly. I will not divulge what you say to me in these private meetings unless or until you tell me I may do so.'*

You understand that, but surely it would make sense if she were to advise you during these private meetings? After all, the other side wouldn't know about it.

'These private meetings are the other reason I will not be offering you any advice on the substance of your case. If either of you thought I was going to do that, you would naturally be very reluctant to confide in me.

'Finally, I would like your agreement to some "ground rules" which usually help proceedings.

'First, I want to ask that only one person speaks at a time, and that he or she is not interrupted.

'Second, however incensed you may feel about what someone has said, you do not resort to physical violence!

'The third ground rule is that if you have any suggestions at any time as to how we should proceed — for example, you might want some time out to go for a walk or something — please tell me. That is really a general rule: this is your mediation and I am here to serve you.'

You are beginning to respect this blend of formality and informality. Although Sally is clearly in control of things, you feel her authority, in some curious way, comes from you.

'Right. If there are no more questions about the process, I suggest we get down to work. I understand that you are here in good faith to achieve a settlement. Is that correct? Are you ready to begin? Perhaps you,' [She's indicating you. Help!] *'would like to begin.'*

★ ★ ★

YOUR OPENING STATEMENT

The purpose of mediation is to get what you want, or at least as much of it as you can get.

An effective opening statement:
- tells the story from your point of view, and sets out the situation as you now understand it;
- acknowledges where your point of view may differ from that of the other side;
- sets out what, again from your point of view, it would take to resolve it;
- sketches the costs and risks of not resolving it through mediation;
- is concise, with no exaggeration; claims are supported by arguments and evidence, and are determined without being aggressive.

If you feel strongly about something, this can be reflected in your opening statement. The other side needs to know that, while you want to reach a settlement and are prepared to be reasonable, you have no intention of renouncing your claim in the face of threats, abuse or manipulation. Spend as much time as you need to prepare the opening statement. If you will have someone with you, rehearse it with them. The crucial thing is to hear it as the other side will hear it, and find a balance between being too conciliatory and too assertive. 'Quietly determined' usually works well.

The key question to ask yourself is:

'What *do* you want?'

This is a Big Question: up there with 'Is there a God?' and 'What's for lunch?' A lot of disputes begin because the answer is not clear, and end when it becomes so.

The following points will help you to clarify what you want and may be equally useful for taking to meetings or, indeed, to carry in your head to help you run your life. Once you can resolve all these points, you will know what you want. Until then you are guessing.

How to Know What You Want

Begin by reading that heading three times:

> 1. How to **KNOW** What You Want
> 2. How to Know What **YOU** want
> 3. How to Know What You **WANT**

It is worth thinking about this.

1. Many people never really discover what they want. They amble around peeking at what everybody else has, and assume that if *others* want it, so must *they*. And if they cannot acquire it by legal means, they may resort to illegal ones. If you *know* what you want, you will not be distracted by the wants of others.

2. And you should not be distracted by the wants of others because they are different from you and therefore want different things. The Golden Rule – *Do unto others as you would have them do unto you* – is fatally flawed. It assumes the others want the same things as you.

3. Finally, lots of people are clearer about what they *don't* want than what they *do* want. It is fine to tell people what you do not want: what you are trying to *avoid* – provided that you have first told them what you want to *achieve*.

The importance of this was brought home to me during some talks between Israelis and Palestinians. While the Palestinians were quite clear about their demands for their own state, the Israelis tended to couch their negotiations in terms of what they were trying to avoid, such as terrorism, economic insecurity, Islamic fundamentalism etc. One of the Palestinians muttered to me during a break: '*It would be so much easier to negotiate with them if we knew what they wanted.*' He was quite right.

The following checklist is designed, first, to help *you* know what you really want, and second, to help you tell the other side during a mediation what you really want. Getting the content right is also the first step to making the communication effective.

> ### 1. State what you want in the *positive*.

As explained above, it is much easier to respond to someone who knows what they do want rather than what they don't. If you practise, you will find that most statements framed in the negative – what you don't want – can with a little ingenuity be reframed into the positive. For example, '*I do not want a relationship with my ex-husband*' could become '*One condition of any agreement is that my ex-husband never contacts me.*' Reframing something into the positive also tends to soften the language you use and how you express yourself, and can therefore sound more reasonable to the other side: '*I don't want your children screaming around in the garden when I am trying to rest!*' somehow sounds much more kill-joy than '*When I am trying to rest I would appreciate it if your children could be quieter.*'

> ### 2. Make what you want *specific*.

If the most important question one ever asks in mediation is '*What do you want?*', the second most important question is '*How will you know when you have it?*' Endless misunderstandings arise from people *thinking* they know what other people mean. When someone says '*I want a car,*' you are really none the wiser. Does it mean they want a brand new Porsche to carve up the motorways? Or an ancient jalopy to take the sheep to market?

That is a simple example. Think of the arguments which have ensued because some politicians say they want a 'federal' Europe without defining what they mean by 'federal'. Using a word such as federal is meaningless unless you also define *how much* of *which powers* are to be devolved to *whom, how, for how long*, and *under what circumstances those powers can be curtailed or revoked*. The foolishness of those who advocate federalism without defining what they mean is matched only by the foolishness of those who contradict them without knowing what they are contradicting.

> ### 3. State *why* you want it.

Things – even quite everyday things – have different meanings in different contexts. A kitchen knife beside a carrot and a chopping board has a different significance from a kitchen knife hefted in the fist of an avenging cuckold. Telling people why you want something also explains your motivation, and gives you the chance to establish the legitimacy of your wanting it, both from your point of view, and theirs. (This is assuming, of course, that what you want *is* legitimate.)

Explaining why you want something also helps others to place a value on what you want. Sums of money, for example, never have a fixed value. That is the sort of statement which sends accountants gibbering to their spreadsheets: but it is true. The value *to you* of any sum of money can only be calculated in relation to why you want it, and how much of it you already have. Think of the contrast between a millionaire and a homeless street person finding a £10 note on the pavement.

In financial mediations turning on calculations of cost and risk, disputants take different risks according to why they want their money. You may settle for a smaller sum, and less risk, if you just want the money for a holiday. If the mediation is your last hope for rescuing a failing business, you may gamble a little harder. Telling the other side *why* you want something helps to explain your actions to them, it may sort out communications failures, and it may also help them to justify to themselves why they should give it to you.

---

4. Say what *you* are prepared to offer to get what you want.

People in disputes quite often start to believe that their opponents, those they hold responsible for the situation, are also solely responsible for resolving it. If the other side believes the same, because they perceive the situation from their point of view, there will be stalemate and inaction. Tell them what you are prepared to do to help resolve the situation. You can do this as a unilateral action and a demonstration of goodwill; or you can suggest a reciprocal action or joint action with them. For example:

A *unilateral* action: '*I am sorry this happened. I would really like to apologize for the situation.*'

107

A *reciprocal* action: '*If you repair my door, I will withdraw my complaint to the housing association.*'
A *joint* action: '*Do you think it would be helpful if we both apologized?*'

On the whole, joint or reciprocal actions are to be preferred over unilateral ones because they help to build a new relationship. On the other hand, sometimes it takes a unilateral action, such as an apology, to unlock a situation and induce movement from others. Perhaps one of the great moral faults and weaknesses of the law is that it can penalize the person who apologizes or admits they were at fault. Both mediators and lawyers are familiar with cases which have mushroomed out of control because a client was advised to say nothing when a straightforward apology would have ended a dispute on the spot.

---

5. Specify the *size* or *scope* of what you want.

People get frightened by what they are asked to do. Demand a large sum of money from someone and they freeze like a rabbit in the headlights: '*That much?*' Then tell them that you are quite prepared to accept their money in instalments, and they sigh with relief.

It is the same with any task you find daunting. Break it down into a series of steps, each one individually quite achievable, and suddenly the impossible becomes possible. In a mediation, when the stresses and uncertainties naturally make things seem even harder than usual, the simple act of breaking down what you want into its component parts will make your demands seem more reasonable and help the other side to relax.

---

6. State what you will do *next*.

Finally, there is a fear in any negotiation that the action you take will not be conclusive: that nothing will happen and, in fact, your willingness to make a move may be interpreted as a sign of weakness to be exploited. You have this fear about them; they have it about you.

A useful way to defuse this is to state, in addition to the step you are making, the step *beyond* it. So, you might say: '*I want to make clear that I will pay £x to resolve this problem. If you agree to this, then I will take no further action in pursuit of my additional claim.*' If there is no further action you can take anyway, then you could say, '*If you agree to this, then we can all go home.*' The aim is to cut out the reluctance to make movements for fear of the 'slippery slope' or the 'thin end of the wedge': both potent reasons why deadlocked situations can be difficult to break out of. Each side fears that any move by them will be perceived as the dam breaking and the prelude to a total collapse. By specifying what will happen a step or two in the future, you keep control of your own moves and, in a curious way, you reassure others.

RESPONDING TO THEIR OPENING STATEMENT

Your opening statement is the last part of the mediation for which you can prepare in this formal sense, because the rest of it will depend to quite a large extent on how well communications develop, how each side responds to the other, and the calculations you make about accepting what is on offer on the table or pushing for a better deal.

★ ★ ★

> People's effectiveness in mediation is determined by two things:
> − *what* they say and
> − *how* they say it;
> and hence the climate they create.

For most parties in dispute, the what, the how and the climate cannot be separated. That is why they need a mediator, and the mediator's job is to achieve those separations by clarifying the content, managing the communication and creating the climate and the opportunity for people to jump off that train to the courthouse. It follows that if the parties could do all those things, the mediator would be redundant. In fact, some mediators describe their role as exactly that: teaching the parties to do those things themselves so that mediation is no longer required.

Just as it is easier to sing with someone who knows the same tune, so it is easier for the mediator to be effective if the clients already understand what makes negotiation harder or easier. One side may not choose the easier way, or they may not choose it until they have given the other side a hard time – and that is fine because sometimes people have been hurt and they need, and have every right, to say so.

Be prepared for the other side to have a go at you, and feel free to have a go at them in turn. If you are outraged by the other side's opening statement, do not be afraid to say so, but bear in mind the following points:

- describe how strongly you feel about what has been said by talking about your *feelings* and *reactions;*
- avoid accusations. Talking about *your* feelings and reactions is legitimate: they will listen to them. If you describe and judge *their* behaviour, they will stop listening and start thinking about why you are wrong;
- even in your rage, say clearly and assertively what you want, and *what you are prepared to do to get it.*

The other side will realize that although you are furious, you are also *rational* and *reasonable.* They will be unable to dismiss your arguments as irrational and unreasonable, and they will have to take you seriously. People defending their own interests tend to be swayed by both reason and emotion. So the purpose of your anger should be to persuade them emotionally that you are right, and to impress on them the determination with which you will pursue your interests.

★   ★   ★

You have got through your opening statement and listened to theirs. Depending on the situation, you may now spend more time together, or the mediator may ask to speak to each of you privately. Whether the next stage in the mediation is joint or separate meetings, you are likely to be required to expand on what you said in your opening statement. The following chapter therefore looks in greater detail at the whole business of communicating effectively.

Chapter 9

Stage 4: Putting Your Case

The opening moves in a mediation do much to establish the climate for at least the next hour or two, and often for very much longer. The more positive the opening moves, the quicker and easier the mediation should be. This chapter sets out what you can do to put your case across effectively, and make the mediation easier, quicker and therefore cheaper.

The following points will help prevent basic failures of communication and enable you to establish a sound working dialogue as early as possible. While they are described here in the context of mediation, they are equally applicable to negotiation, or indeed to any situation in which communication is important.

COMMUNICATION IS A TWO-WAY PROCESS

The quality of your communication can only be determined by the response you generate. The upshot of this is that you should never say to anyone, '*You do not understand me!*' because the responsibility for their understanding you — or not — is yours, not theirs.

So what do you do when you have made something as clear as you can — and the other person is still not getting your point? Simple: you say it again, differently, and you go on saying it in different ways until you get through to them. The reason for this is also simple: if you place on *them* the responsibility for understanding *you*, then you effectively cede control of your own communications. You are giving them the right to interpret your communications not as you intend them to be interpreted, but as they choose to interpret them. And they will: they will distort them to mean what they want them to mean — probably to your disadvantage. You can watch and hear this happen on any radio or television debate, and observe the frustration and anger which results from it:

what is *said* is not necessarily *heard*,
what is *heard* is not always *understood*, as it is intended to be, and therefore what is *understood* is not always *accepted*.

To complicate things further, this failure of communication may not be recognized by either party. Why is it so difficult to communicate?

THE COMMON CAUSES OF COMMUNICATIONS FAILURES

There is a blend of cognitive and behavioural psychology which goes under the forbidding name of *Neuro-Linguistic Programming* – or NLP as a much-needed abbreviation. NLP uses something called the *Meta Model* to explain how communications between people go wrong. The Meta Model is based on the observation that the language human beings use in order to communicate with each other becomes progressively more detached from the experience it represents as that experience becomes deeper or more complex to convey. In other words, to avoid communication becoming overburdened we simplify everything. NLP says the three universal methods of simplification are:

1. **Deletion**: we leave things out;
2. **Distortion**: by leaving things out;, we unintentionally distort what remains; and
3. **Generalization**: we further simplify by generalizing, in order to avoid spelling out every condition and exception.

These mechanisms are essential for fluent communication, and they also make certain activities possible. Training and education, for example, would be impossible if we did not generalize.

Unfortunately, because we all delete, distort and generalize *differently,* our efforts to make ourselves understood may have unintended consequences. For example, something is deleted by one side because it is regarded as irrelevant; but it may be highly valued by the other side. So, says NLP, many of the misunderstandings that arise between people are the consequence of an entirely natural process of language selection without which communication would be impossible.

NLP's Meta Model provides a sequence of questions designed to replace deleted information, reshape what has been distorted, and make specific what has been generalized. It provides a useful checklist of points for helping to unravel whatever may be preventing good communication. One word of caution before using them. Deletion, distortion and generalization may be general human tendencies, but how the individual uses them is a personal matter. Challenging them can be experienced as aggressive, pedantic, and intrusive. It is essential to question them indirectly and gently, using softening phrases such as '*I wonder . . .*' or '*I am curious to know how . . .*' Do not use them in such a way that the other person thinks you are picking apart their words merely for your idle amusement.

When you are having trouble getting your points across to the other side, look for the following problems:

Deletions

1. **Unspecified nouns**: for example, the sentence '*The community is outraged,*' is often used in the press.
   - Ask **what** community, **who specifically** is this community?
2. **Unspecified verbs**: for example, following on the above:
   - **How specifically** is the community outraged?
3. **Comparisons**: often used in isolation and disguised as adverbs, such as in '*The meeting went badly.*'
   - Ask *badly* **compared with** what?
4. **Judgments**: often hiding inside adverbs: '*This policy is clearly wrong.*'
   - Ask *clearly* **to whom**? And **on what grounds**?
5. **Nominalizations:** the interesting process by which words which describe processes are turned into nouns,

and in the course of it lose their meaning. A good example is *education*.
– Ask **who** is educating **whom, about what**, *and how*?

Nominalizations are probably the single most dangerous language pattern because they subvert meaning so insidiously and so silently. Other examples of common nominalizations are *government, respect, discipline, specification, punishment, justice* and so on. All of them are useful shorthand because we think we know what we mean by them, but these meanings may not be shared. So two business people may be arguing about a disputed specification without realising that 'specification' may mean different things to each. Nominalizations are also fostered by elites, professions and even whole cultures to give the illusion of being special, and to give an impression of emotional invulnerability – because nominalizations always depersonalize experience.

Generalizations

6. **Possibility words** such as *can, cannot, possible, impossible*. These are words used by people to deny capability, when what they are really seeking is to avoid choice. For example, somebody says '*I cannot do that,*' when what they mean is '*I do not want to do that.*'
   – Ask '*what would happen if you did . . . ?*' or '*what stops you?*'
7. *Necessity words* such as *should, should not, ought, must* etc. They imply the existence of some set of rules or sanctions, but these are never specified, and, again, they are mechanisms for limiting choice and behaviour.
   – Ask '*who says?*' or '*what would happen if you did?*'
8. **Universal** words used to generalize, such as *all, always, never, none, every*. They are potent substitutes for thought and discrimination; they encourage prejudice, narrow-mindedness and ignorance. (They also have their uses: '*smoking is always risky.*')
   – Ask about *exceptions* to them.

Distortions

9. **Unjustified linkage:** ideas or statements linked in such

115

a way that they are taken to mean the same thing. For example, in a family mediation, somebody saying '*You forgot Johnny's birthday . . . you do not love him as much as I do.*'

10. **Presuppositions**: the danger of these is well known to every defence lawyer whose client is asked '*Why don't you stop beating your wife/husband?*' *Why* questions are only one way of disguising presuppositions. Others are sentences containing *since*, *when*, *if* or verbs such as *ignore*, *realize*, or *be aware*. For example, '*You ignore a red light at your peril*' implies that it has been ignored.
    – Challenge by filling in the presupposition.

11. **Cause and Effect**: perhaps a cultural as well as a linguistic phenomenon, this denotes the linear thinking which tends to link things causally when they should not be. For example, '*The fog caused the accident*,' when fog cannot wrestle cars into colliding with each other.
    – Ask '*How – specifically . . .*' the one causes the other.

12. **Mind Reading**: this is another potent source of conflict, and comes in two types. In the first, someone assumes they know what another person is thinking or feeling, as in '*You are angry with me.*' The other is the mirror of the first: '*You should have known how I would feel about that.*' In both these cases knowledge of a person's thinking is being presumed, and that can be insulting and provocative.
    – Ask '*how specifically do you know/could I have known . . . ?*'

At first glance these points may look rather theoretical and complicated. Read them through twice, and I guarantee you will begin to remember instances in which arguments incorporating deletions, distortions and generalizations have been used against you. Look out for them, question them, and be prepared to challenge them: it will increase your ability to influence the other side. The more effectively you learn to communicate, the more easily you will achieve what you need to.

HOW TO INFLUENCE PEOPLE WITHOUT ANNOYING THEM

The keys to effective influence can be boiled down to a number of basic principles:

1. Listen *actively* and *accurately*.

It may seem paradoxical to start instructions for communicating with listening: but this is the beginning of good communication for you as well as for the mediator. The next time you listen to a speech, a sermon or a documentary programme on radio or television, wait for half an hour and then write down all you can remember. You will probably be unpleasantly surprised by how little you actually absorbed.

 — Listen for where things are going wrong: for the deletions, distortions and generalizations, so that you can clear up any past failures of communication;
 — Listen for the content of what others say, so that you know what they want even if they do not express it as clearly as you;
 — Listen for the tones in which they do it: try to discover from their tone of voice which issues are the most sensitive, where they feel less sure, where they feel particularly strongly;
 — Listen for particular words or phrases they use, and use them yourself to show that you are listening.

When they have finished speaking, ask them if there is anything else they would like to say before you respond. No, don't say it sarcastically — '*Are you* sure *you have finished?*' Say it in a way which tells them that you are genuinely concerned to hear what they have to say, and that you want to know more about the situation from their point of view. Ask questions. '*Could you please tell me a bit more about . . . ? I want to make sure I understand clearly how you see that point.*' Send the message that you are not at all the monster they imagine you to be, but a totally reasonable person who is open to a reasonable solution. You can do all this without in any way weakening your own case.

> 2. Speak *clearly* and *purposefully*.

The basic advice for making any speech also holds good for mediation:

- tell 'em what you are going to say; tell 'em; then tell 'em what you have said;
- secondly, break up what you say into clear sections, with a title for each, and break up each section into sequences of no more than three points. This makes it easier for people to make notes and follow your argument;
- finally, tell a story. Start with some background so that people can get the present situation into perspective. Then describe what has happened from your point of view and make it clear that that is what you are doing by using phrases such as *'I understood this to mean that . . .'*

Do not think that taking trouble over telling your story is pandering to the other side. Telling the story as well as you can, making it balanced, making it clear that you are not trying to impose your version on them: these are all ways to get them to understand why you feel the way you do.

> 3. Welcome new information.

Didn't someone once say that the first sign of wisdom is recognizing the depth of one's own ignorance? People in dispute have excellent reasons for concealing their ignorance and resisting new information: it may undermine a whole, carefully prepared case or endanger a cherished stereotype. But the alternative to accepting new information is to retreat into a fantasy world in which things are how we want them to be rather than how they really are. There are plenty of such people around, convincing themselves that communism works, or that there are no dangers to our global environment, or that the other side really intended to destroy their company when they unintentionally supplied faulty equipment.

Stay open to new information. Make it clear that you welcome the other side's perception of the problem, and that if they can convince you that they are right – *on the merits of the situation and on the evidence they have* – then you will be happy to accept what they say. This brings us to the next point.

---

4. Be open to persuasion.

Remaining open-minded on an issue is sensible for several reasons:

- there is always the possibility that, having heard the other side's arguments, you will want to change your mind. If you have always indicated this possibility, to do so is less of a climbdown;
- to be open-minded is a sign of strength rather than weakness: it is only the weak and the insecure who refuse to listen;
- to be open-minded is to imply respect for the other side, and respecting them is one way of getting them to respect you.

This final point leads to the next general principle for getting your arguments across.

---

5. Try to respect others even when – perhaps *especially* when – you disagree with them.

All relationships, to work at all, demand respect. As soon as a mediation is agreed, the relationship with the other side is different. Up until then, you may have been content to regard and treat them as the enemy, but now you have something in common, something which needs to be built on if that agreement is to extend to the things which divide you. Respect begins by accepting the right of the other person to differ, with an equal right to be heard and to be taken seriously.

Demonstrating your respect for the other person helps create a positive climate for the mediation, and paves the way for them to respect you. There are a number of things you can do unilaterally to start this process:

- treat them with courtesy: fetch chairs, pour coffee, pass sugar. People notice little things;
- make it clear that you intend to direct your efforts at solving the problem rather than attacking them personally;
- let them know that you respect their right to perceive the situation differently, and show an interest in why they do so. If you come from different social or cultural backgrounds, explain how your background influences your understanding of the situation;
- accept the right of others to have feelings. You may feel they are unnecessarily emotional about what to you is a trivial point: but if it matters a lot to them — then it matters, and you need to respect their feelings about it;
- acknowledge the right of people not to like you.

During preparation for a recent mediation, one side wanted to say in their opening statement, that they hoped to create a new friendship between the parties. Given that both sides were sworn enemies, I advised strongly against this. It was hardly credible to express such a hope before anything had changed between them; and I knew that the other side had absolutely no desire to kiss and make up, let alone become friends. They just wanted to solve the problem. You have to accept the other side's right not to like or trust you, or even to be polite. Aim to establish a working relationship with the other side: just good enough to enable you to work together long enough to find a mutually acceptable solution to your problem. (If part of that solution is a better relationship, then obviously you have to work that much harder.) Beyond that, any improvement in the relationship is a bonus.

One of the approaches often advocated in mediation and negotiation is to 'separate the people from the problem'. In practice this can be difficult because sometimes the people *are* the problem. What is sometimes possible is making some separation between their *behaviour* and the problem. You can do this by saying things like, '*I accept that you feel strongly about this situation, and I understand that is why you heaved a brick through my window. While I deplore your approach, I am prepared to work with you to find a better way to sort things out between us.'* If what you really want to do is respond to them in kind, that is the moment to separate *your* behaviour from the problem.

RESPONDING TO ANGER

Of all the communications blockers, anger is one of the most potent. It can be useful to be mentally prepared for the anger which may be directed at you. If you are prepared, you are more likely to choose a response which advances rather than impedes progress. The following points may help your preparation.

1. Anger is nearly always a *substitute* emotion as well as the expression of honest rage: it is a symptom of other feelings. When someone gets angry, take time to listen and discover the real sources of their anger.
2. Anger is often self-directed, even when it is expressed at others. Find out why people might be angry with themselves. What have they done or failed to do?
3. Anger is sometimes the last-ditch effort to avoid taking responsibility. Find out what the person needs in order to do what they have to do.
4. If anger is making progress difficult, try to identify some small, trivial cause of it which might be resolved quite easily. Interrupt and suggest a solution. This may break the escalation.
5. Never dismiss anger as irrational: you may overlook a genuine but deeply buried problem.
6. On the other hand, feigning anger is a negotiating ploy to intimidate the opposition. If you suspect this is the case, ask what specifically is the cause of the person getting so angry.

We flip into anger because it is easier, less complicated, than admitting to ourselves, let alone to others, our confusions, frustrations, insecurities. Anger is a particularly masculine emotion: so much easier to get into a fury and blame everyone else rather than having to face up to one's own feelings. Women, by contrast, tend to be brought up to see anger as 'unfeminine'. Their anger can become turned inward against themselves and be expressed as guilt and self-disgust. You should not interpret all this to mean, however, that anger is necessarily 'bad'. It may be essential for people to get their shouting done before they can make progress. If you find yourself getting angry during a mediation, there are three things you can do to make your anger productive:

1. Direct it at the problem rather than the other people.
2. Expressing anger while you feel angry makes you even angrier. If you feel you are going to really explode, it is better — for you and the mediation — to ask for a break.
3. Make the cause of your anger explicit. Don't just yell about the other side being a bunch of crooks; tell them: '*I am furious because I had received an undertaking that the widgets would be here by Friday 13th. They did not arrive, and I lost an important contract as a result.*'

Note the wording of the above. Not '*you failed to deliver on time*' but '*I had received an undertaking . . .*' It is always legitimate to express your own feelings about something. As soon as you start talking about the behaviour of others they will stop listening to you, and your point will be lost.

CHOOSING THE WAY TO SUCCESS

Many people approach a dispute as if it is beyond the control of those who are party to it. This comforting denial of responsibility can contribute to escalation of the problem. Implicit in mediation is the recognition that disputes happen the way they do because of the procedural and behavioural choices made by those involved. These are usually lumped together by mediators under the general heading of *process choices*. In every mediation there are process choices which help make it successful, and others which make success more elusive. One of the most important roles of a mediator is to use *process skills* to ensure the clients make the most productive process choices. This is one of the subtlest aspects of intervening in conflict, and the one which is most often overlooked by those who have no formal training in mediation.

A conscious choice to lower the intensity of conflict may not in itself make a mediation successful, but it is often the essential first step towards the parties working together sufficiently to explore the possibilities of settlement. The following columns contrast process choices which tend to escalate conflict with those which tend to reduce it.

The dispute will be *harder* to resolve if you:	The dispute will be *easier* to resolve if you:
— start with *your* solution and insist it is the only one	— start by outlining the issues
— make extravagant claims and ignore the interests of others	— explain what you need to achieve and why
— tell people what you want	— ask others what they want
— set deadlines	— explore time constraints for yourself and others
— are aggressive	— are assertive
— focus only on the short term	— focus on the short term and the longer term
— ignore relationships	— take relationships into account as appropriate
— address issues narrowly and shallowly	— address issues broadly and deeply
— blame the other side for everything	— encourage appropriate and objective allocation of responsibility
— limit the acceptable options for settlement	— widen the options and constantly seek new ones
— personalize the issues	— address the issues objectively
— insult the other side	— respect the other side
— concentrate on differences and polarize the issues	— look for common ground and build on areas of agreement
— raise your own expectations and lower those of others	— ensure all expectations are realistic
— conceal and withhold resources from the other side	— offer resources and assistance where appropriate

That last one is usually too much for the person who fancies himself or herself as a 'hard' negotiator. Help the other side? You must be kidding! But what if helping the other person is what it takes to solve the problem and end the dispute? Being 'hard' is neither clever nor really tough if as a result you do not get what you want. It isn't wimpish to use your time and skills to understand the needs and concerns of others: there is a difference between understanding and acceptance. Nor is the talk-tough line always the harder one. The contrast between these two approaches is not between 'hard' and 'soft': it is between unproductive and productive. If you want to bash the opposition: fine – but don't then complain if you cannot reach an agreement.

In one situation in which I was involved the tension was rising and rising. It eventually reached a crucial pitch and one of the participants, a young man defending his company's interests, found himself with a clear choice to make. He could either put his case even more strongly, as he thought, by responding to the other side's threats with a dire threat of his own; or he could do something to make the process more productive. He chose the first, easier option. The tension rose higher still and progress became impossible. I asked why he had made that choice. '*I had to*,' he replied. '*They threatened me, so I had to threaten them.*'

No. He did not *have* to do that. He made a *choice* to do it, and he had to live with the consequences. Human beings are adept at finding other people to blame. The only person whose choices and behaviour you can control is your own. It may be tempting to give as good as you get, to return the insult, to be sarcastic, to do the threatening and bluffing. You have a perfect right to do these things – and you also have the opportunity to make other, more productive choices.

★ ★ ★

Before you can make those choices, however, you need to understand as well as you can what is going on in your situation. The next couple of chapters are about disputes in general: what goes on beneath all the sound and fury.

Chapter 10

Stage 5: Exploring the Situation

Let us begin by identifying some key words for understanding what conflict stems from.

Conflict springs from . . .	
CAUSES:	How people initiate, manage or respond to
TRIGGERS:	*differences* or *changes*
COMMUNICATION:	in their *communication*, *understanding* or *perceptions* of how others are challenging their
FUEL:	*needs* and *interests*, *territory*, *values* and *principles*, *expectations*, calculations of *risks and uncertainties*, their *information*, their sense of *power, control*, and *legitimacy*, and therefore affecting people's current *relationships, behaviour* and sense of *identity*.

So understanding how conflict has arisen and what to do about it means first identifying:
- the underlying CAUSES;
- then the immediate TRIGGER factors of difference and/or change;

— how these are being COMMUNICATED; and then
— the subjects, issues or factors which are providing the FUEL for the conflict.

We will examine each of these parts in turn to give an overview of how they fit together and how a mediator approaches them.

CAUSES

Facts and issues do not of themselves cause conflict: people do. Talking solely about issues can sometimes obscure human responsibility for them. Saying the war in the Falklands was about the issue of sovereignty could imply that it was somehow an objective matter of history, like a famine or a flood, over which human beings had no control. What actually caused the war was Argentinian behaviour, to which the British responded in kind. This may seem a minor distinction, but it matters if you are to separate *symptoms* from *causes*. The invasion was a symptom of political and diplomatic failure; the cause was poor decision-making as a result of domestic pressures on the Argentinian junta, and misjudgments about the likely British response. Something similar is happening when people say that a clause in a business contract has caused a dispute. If the relationship between those who have entered into the contract is good enough, the clause may cause a problem until it is sorted out, but it is the people involved and the quality of their relationship which determines whether or not a problem turns into a dispute.

Too often people treat the symptoms rather than the causes of conflict, rather as doctors, or at least Western-trained doctors, are sometimes inclined to treat the symptoms of an illness rather than look for its deeper causes. The legal system also tends to encourage this. I find it useful when discussing a case with a solicitor to find out *who exactly* did *what exactly* rather than relying on deletions such as "There was a breach of contract".

TRIGGERS

1. Change

All conflict is about achieving or resisting change. To understand any conflict situation better you can do worse than look for *who* is being asked to change *what,* the *cost* of it, and *when* and *how* that cost should be met (understanding that *cost* here does not necessarily or only mean money: the cost may be measured in terms of stress, or emotional damage, or personal distress). Managing conflict often means managing change; resolving conflict often means resolving the problems created by change.

Those who are enthusiastic for change do not always appreciate its consequences from other people's points of view. Giving those others a chance to explain what change means to them is often helpful. Change is also a prime source of uncertainty which, if left unresolved, causes fear and then hostility.

2. Differences

All conflicts arise out of differences: so much is obvious. Harder to define, sometimes, is which differences really count. Checking through the list of factors which fuel conflict helps people to identify precisely where it is they differ. Husband and wife: '*We love each other. We want the same things. Why is our relationship going wrong? Ah yes: different values. You believe in monogamy; I want an open marriage.*'

Discovering in what ways people are different from each other can tell you much about what has gone wrong between them. Sometimes even seemingly trivial differences can have serious consequences. Larger differences, such as those arising between people of different races or cultures, can provide the triggers for catastrophe as we have seen all too often in recent years.

Differences acknowledged, discussed, understood, respected and perhaps laughed about, need not trigger conflict, though they will always retain the potential to do so. One seasoned mediator, faced with a rip-roaring partnership dispute, pulled out a personality profile test and insisted the warring partners complete it on the spot. The test results revealed profound differences of personality, and suggested that the partners had all been doing the wrong jobs. It did not resolve the immediate issues in dispute, but it defused much of their anger and gave them some insight into how their problems had arisen.

The trigger to conflict is the specific incident which sets in motion a sequence of events, emotions or reactions. The major triggers are changes and differences. Changes trigger conflict because they are stressful, they increase uncertainties, and they undermine the stability of a situation. Differences trigger conflict when they reach a certain point: we can all live with some degree of difference between ourselves and others, but there comes a point when these differences, like changes, become too much for us to handle. When this happens, we perceive these differences or changes as the cause of our discomfort – and try to resolve or suppress them. But, of course, these changes and differences are not in themselves the causes: the real causes are the people whose needs and fears lead them to want change or difference.

COMMUNICATIONS

So many things in both conflict and its resolution come back to communication and its offspring, and I make no apology for an element of repetition about them. These are the primary engines of conflict, but they are more complicated than they look. You sometimes hear people saying of some well-known situation being reported on the news, '*If only they'd get around the table they could clear up this misunderstanding and the dispute would be over.*' This springs from the 'all conflict is a mistake' school of thought. It introduces the notions of *mis*communication, *mis*understanding, *mis*perception.

These are dangerous nonsenses because they shift responsibility from the communicator to the recipient. A communication which fails does not produce a misunderstanding: it produces an understanding which is different from what was intended. That is an important difference. Likewise, there is no such thing as a misperception: there are just perceptions which, for better or worse, are simply what somebody perceives. If you come at me with a hatchet my perception will be that you are threatening my life, and I will take whatever action is required to defend myself. I am not responsible for knowing that you were only going to chop wood: it was up to you to make it clear that that was your intention. The problem was not my perception, but your action.

The real problems arise not when people fail to communicate or to understand each other, but communicate and understand all too well. For example, one person demands something which another person refuses to give. No misunderstanding there: conflict stems out of very precise understanding. Nor can people be blamed for putting the worst interpretation on an action.

British or American tanks arriving in Kuwait are perceived differently from Iraqi tanks arriving in Kuwait for very sound reasons. Perceptions are just perceptions; they are not right or wrong, accurate or inaccurate. To think otherwise is to encourage sloppy thinking, acting and communicating.

Failures of communication, failures of understanding, and actions intended one way but perceived differently are relatively easy to resolve in mediation. The mediator intervenes to ensure that what is communicated is received and understood in the way it was intended, or asks questions which reveal how a perfectly innocent action by one party might be perceived by another to have a more sinister meaning.

FUEL

1. Needs, Interests and Territory

These are the *commodities* people want: land, money, reputation, apologies, power. Needs and interests represent, to those who want them, material gain. They may also be symbols of other things. The Falkland Islands, for example, are symbols of national pride and sovereignty for Argentina. So although commodities are primarily material things, they may also have non-material meaning and value.

Territory is both a literal and a psychological source of conflict. If you have ever met someone who guards their 'patch', whether it is ordering the stationery in an organization, their allotment, or their car, you will know how jealously territory can be defended. The reasons are simple. People's sense of their territory is powerfully linked to their sense of personal identity. Coupled to this is the sense of personal boundaries we all have, and here cultural differences may again be a factor.

Territory becomes particularly important in a time of change because it represents security. The psychologist Donald Winnicott coined the term *transitional object* to describe the things to which children become deeply attached, such as teddy bears, blankets or even wooden spoons. Experience suggests that the stress and insecurity of conflict can cause adults to regress and invest in transitional objects. Territory is an ancient and obvious one. We can literally or symbolically build walls around ourselves and keep the hostile world outside.

Objections to change, reluctance to cede control, bureaucracy, people taking on extra responsibilities, demanding trivial perks and privileges, or insisting on minor points of principle or protocol – these are the symptoms of territorial conflict. Mediators respond to them by helping those involved to feel secure in the process, and then by separating each symptom out from the main part of the dispute and dealing with it on its merits.

2. Values and Principles

Values and principles cover the non-material elements in conflict, such as religious beliefs, political ideologies, and moral values. There may however be some overlap with material needs and interests: a political principle may have a material expression. Britain fought Argentina to establish the vital principle that international banditry should not prevail. We also wanted our rocks back.

There are some points to remember when dealing with matters of value and principle. (People often define principles and values differently, but I have yet to find a straightforward and convincing way to define the difference. I use them interchangeably here to mean something of abstract rather than material importance to someone.) First, when *challenged*, principles *may* be expressed more strongly than they are felt; second, principles are often invoked to cloak or to justify less worthy causes; third, the more abstract the principle, the more important it is to establish its real significance to the person who holds it, preferably by asking for concrete examples.

Finally, the fact that principles often become reduced to easily-repeated slogans and catchphrases can persuade people that they are not 'real'. For this reason it is always a good idea to make them concrete and to establish who is defending them, because principles vary somewhat according to who is quoting them. Without being too cynical, it is useful to believe that non-negotiable principles *are* in fact negotiable providing you can discover the right currency and the right way to negotiate them. It is always critical, when dealing with questions of principle, to keep one eye on the party's need to justify any compromise to their constituency.

A good example of this was the approach of Terry Waite, envoy to the then Archbishop of Canterbury, during his mission to Libya in January 1985 to mediate the release of four British hostages from Colonel Qaddafi. Waite made judicious references to the Koran and to Qaddafi's own religious principles throughout his mission. The Libyan leader, for whom the hostages were liable to become a political embarrassment, saw the opportunity to justify to his supporters the release of the hostages on religious and humanitarian grounds. (The Colonel's religious principles had not, of course, prevented him from taking the hostages in the first place.) Waite's intervention enabled both the Libyan and the British governments to dispose of the problem without having to make politically unacceptable concessions.

3. Expectations

Expectations are a potent source of conflict because of the frustration when they are unfulfilled or are fulfilled differently from how people anticipated. Expectations are powerful not only because of what is involved physically and materially, but because they are also the outward signs of the unspoken and unconscious *psychological contracts* we establish with other people. The very fact that these contracts, the expectations which we have of each other, are unspoken and unconscious should alert us to their potential for wreaking havoc. Marriage is a good example. Most of us do not set out in detail what we expect of the other person when we get married. We assume that knowing, liking and loving each other will enable us encompass anything our partner might do. But how well can we ever really know another person? What is more, we change, and they change, and our expectations of each other change. These changes can destroy the marriage unless the psychological contract we have established is flexible enough to withstand them. Yet we are mostly unaware of this contract and its terms; the surprise should not be that so many marriages end in divorce, but that so few do.

All relationships involve psychological contracts and the expectations that go with them. Violate them, even unintentionally, and you are in trouble: think of the individual who fails to display sufficient 'team spirit' in an organization or a sports club. Violate them intentionally — lying, abuse, vandalism, and crime are all behaviours which cut across the unconscious expectations human beings have of other human beings even if they do not know them — and society takes a very dim view of you.

131

Mediators often find it useful to discover what expectations people have had of each other, how they have or have not been fulfilled in the past, and how they are expected to be fulfilled in the present and future. Often these expectations have been obscured by poor communication, consequent misunderstandings, and the violations of trust which arise from them.

4. Risk, Uncertainty and Information

Risk and uncertainties provide fuel for conflict because people calculate and try to resolve them differently. How they do this depends on the information they use, so the accuracy of this can also contribute to resolving or escalating the situation.

Quite apart from the influence of different information sources, people seem to have some general perceptions of what is more risky, or less risky.

People seem to perceive situations to be **less risky** *when they are:*	People seem to perceive situations to be **more risky** *when they are:*
Voluntary	Involuntary
Familiar	Unfamiliar
Controllable	Uncontrollable
Fair	Unfair
Chronic	Acute
Unspecific	Specific
Immediate	Delayed
Natural	Unnatural

Problems arise when people assess these factors differently. Think, for example, of how different people calculate the risks associated with nuclear power and the information they seek and use to make these calculations. So you could say that the actions which fuel disputes hinge on people's calculations of the risks of different ways forward. Look at the questions which people commonly ask themselves. What are the chances of losing in court? What are the consequences if we do? What are the chances of winning on appeal? These are questions to which answers can, in principle, be computed if you have the necessary information to limit the range of uncertainties with which to wrestle. You cannot prepare for every eventuality in mediation, but you should not go into it without as much information as you need to make some basic calculations around the uncertainties, costs and risks involved: do I take what the other side is offering? Or do I hold out for more – taking the risk that the mediation will fail and we will end up in court and I may lose?

5. Power, Control and Legitimacy

Power is not in itself 'good' or 'bad', nor a source of conflict. It all depends on how it is used. It becomes a source of conflict when:

- it prevents people doing what needs to be done;
- it coerces people into doing things which do not take account of their needs and interests;
- it *threatens* either of the above.

In my experience, the *fear* of coercion is as great a source of conflict as the fact of it, perhaps because the next step from fear is loss of **control**. Loss of control of one's own destiny is one of the greatest sources of stress, unhappiness and conflict there is. The distribution of power and control is crucial in disputes, and mediation often succeeds because it can help people to avoid a power struggle, so Chapter 11 will explore this whole area at length.

Legitimacy is more than legality. *Legality* concerns the matter of right and wrong according to law. *Legitimacy* concerns people's sense of fairness and reasonableness, conforming to what they conceive as normal conduct. Legitimacy becomes a source of conflict when people perceive it in different ways, or perceive a lack of it. For example, in a negotiation with an insurance company over payment of compensation after a burglary, you are more likely to be successful if your claim appears legitimate in the eyes of the loss adjuster. 'Legitimate' here means not just accurate, but credible, consistent, realistic. If you make extravagant and clearly excessive demands for all sorts of things you cannot prove you ever had, the legitimacy of your entire claim is liable to be questioned. On the other hand, if you can support your claim for your diamond tiara by providing a photograph of you wearing it, the legitimacy of your claim – and therefore your negotiating power – will be substantially increased.

6. Behaviour, Identity and Relationships

This final fuel for the bonfire brings us back almost to the beginning of the cycle: because people's relationships, sense of identity and habits of behaviour determine how they initiate or respond to the triggers we discussed earlier, how they communicate, what is important to them . . . and so on. Conflict is a system in which all the various parts relate to each other. Volumes have been written on the contribution of people's behaviour, identity and relationships to conflict, and you will find some of the fruits of that work duly pillaged and scattered throughout this book. Let me make just one general point about relationships and identity as sources of conflict.

I believe (although I have no evidence beyond observation and experience to support this) that in the West, compared with other cultures, we tend to emphasize our personal needs and identity at the expense of our relationships with other individuals, or with our community, or with society as a whole. Even the wealth of books and magazines devoted to helping us to have perfect partnerships, raise wonderful children and become more interpersonally sensitive, seem ultimately to focus on what's in it for *me* rather than *thee*.

My personal view apart, I think it is generally true to say that the tides of fashion and change in recent years have left people profoundly confused about what constitutes 'normality' in relation to identity, relationships, and behaviour. The waning of the 1980s' emphasis on the individual and the waxing of the supposedly 'caring' 1990s; the gradual shift in traditional gender roles; the decline of marriage: all these leave people not quite knowing how things should be, what to do in any situation, where the new boundaries lie. One of the results of this confusion is conflict. Where boundaries shift and expectations change, disputes will inevitably follow. Through mediation people can in safety begin to appreciate what boundaries have been crossed, what relationships and expectations have been violated, what senses of identity have been affronted.

* * *

Not every situation is going to involve the porridge of issues described above, and some situations are going to be naturally easier than others to resolve. What makes them easier – or harder? The following box, based on work done by the Institute for Conflict Analysis and Resolution, summarizes the factors which will ease or complicate your mediation.

	AGREEMENT IS . . .	
EASIER when there are:		**HARDER** when there are no:
	shared interests	
	shared ambitions	
	shared needs	
	shared fears	
	shared personal values	
	shared maps of the world	
	shared general principles	
when it is clear:		when it is not clear:
	what the issues are	
	who the parties are	
	what they want	
	what procedures are already in place	
	what the options are for resolution	
when there are no complicating factors such as:		when there are complicating factors such as:
	lack of preparation	
	high stakes	
	deeply-rooted differences	
	multiple parties	
	many issues	
	contradictory incentives for each side	
	limited options	
	time constraints	
	inadequate resources	

The mediator's job is to use devices like the above to help both sides understand the dispute, and what makes it difficult to resolve.

★ ★ ★

This chapter has set out some of the understanding of conflict which the mediator will use to help you and the other side appreciate better what is going on. The next chapter looks at how the mediator will help you avoid a power struggle with the other side.

Chapter 11

Stage 6: Avoiding Power Struggles

In all the many presentations, talks, training courses and consultancy assignments I have done around the subject of conflict, the one issue which is guaranteed to come up time and again is that of power. More precisely, it is the question of power differences; when you really get down to it, what people really want to know is *'What do I do if the other side is more powerful than me?'* and *'Can the mediator really make a difference?'* To answer these questions we have to look more closely at power and how it works, and the role of the mediator in situations where the power is unevenly distributed.

GENERAL APPROACH

There are circumstances in which the disparities of power in the situation will make it difficult to reach a win-win solution, or a solution which is sustainable. There is always the temptation for the more powerful party to impose its solution even if that is not the best one. In such situations the basic role of the mediator is to ensure that power is not the only determining factor in the outcome, and that the power available is directed at achieving a realistic solution rather than crushing the other side. If there are vast disparities of power between those in conflict, it is unlikely that the situation will come to mediation anyway. Mediation is more likely to happen if each side perceives the other as more powerful, or where each side wields totally different types of power, and therefore neither side can compute the risks of winning or losing. For this reason the matter of risk has to be considered together with power.

This chapter begins with some general points about power,

differentiates between power and *capability*, reviews the matter of risk, and then sets out how a mediator uses the mediation process so that power is used constructively to achieve a sustainable solution. Finally, it looks at some ways you can safeguard yourself in a mediation where you feel that superior power is being used against you.

ANALYSING POWER

Power comes in many forms: the power of position, of resources, of expertise, even of the charismatic personality. But these days it is rarely monolithic. The warlords and absolute rulers are, with some notable exceptions, confined to dominating families, small organizations or small countries. On the whole the age of tyrants is over. In the late twentieth century a number of factors conspire to rob them of their absolute rule.

Organizations, for example, are moving away from the old hierarchies which are slow and cumbersome in a world which works faster and faster. 'Flatter' management structures and more devolution of responsibility lead to a fragmentation of power and a reliance on collaboration rather than autocracy to get things done. Likewise, people are recognizing that the talents of individuals are increasingly adding value and distinctiveness to organizations, so individuals are 'empowered' by having more access to information, and being consulted more about their work. This is also happening in society as a whole. The growth of democracy around the world and greater concern for the rights of individuals over those of élites mean that relationships, whether between management and workers, parents and children or police and citizens depend more on consent and less on *diktat*.

This process is far from complete; and at times it proceeds fitfully and uncertainly as the powers of yesterday make last-ditch attempts to preserve their right to rule. It is also true that as the powerful recognize this general trend, they make many efforts to disguise the power they wield. Equally, at the same time as ordinary people are expecting to be empowered, so the divisions between the empowered and the disempowered become increasingly acute. In time perhaps the powerful will recognize that it is actually easier to deal with people who are empowered, and can meet them on a level playing field, than it is to suppress the ambitions of those who have nothing to lose by tearing up the turf. Anyway, the upshot of this gradual shift in power and perceptions of power is that a lot of people who, in the past, would have steamrollered their way through any opposition to their ambitions or demands, now feel incapable of doing so – or perhaps too embarrassed to try.

So the first point to remember if you are faced with a powerful adversary is to realize that things may not be as bleak as they seem. The next step is to look at what is the nature of the power you fear. There are five types of power which commonly affect negotiations and mediations:

---

1. Physical: as exercised by armies, or by people in large numbers;
2. Economic: as held by (some) governments, large businesses and institutions, people in large numbers, people who are rich;
3. Information: as used by people and institutions who have information denied to others, or who can use information to sway opinions;
4. Emotional: held by those who are in a position to manipulate the feelings of others;
5. Education: the power held by those in a position to help others to greater understanding.

The effectiveness of these five types of power depends on the person or situation on which they are impacting, as well as on the skill and judgment with which they are wielded. In fact, power should always be measured at its point of *impact* rather than at its source. For example:

– one side cannot know the value of its physical strength without knowing that of its opponent;
– one side may have more resources than the other, but those resources may be in the wrong place, or of the wrong kind;
– the information held by one party is only valuable if the other has a similar estimation of its importance;
– the value of any action against the other side is relative to the other side's ability to deflect or sidestep it.

At its point of impact, power may be felt to coerce, induce, or persuade, with the exception of educational power which relies for its impact upon the active co-operation of its recipient. Agreement reached by coercion or inducement, i.e. bullying or bribing, is likely to be resented as unfair, illicit, or shaming, and therefore may be only temporary: a regular problem with agreements reached by hard bargaining tactics. Agreement by persuasion may be productive or not, depending on the means and degree of persuasion.

People tend to become mesmerized by the idea of superior power and, like the rabbit caught in the headlights, freeze in dreadful anticipation of being squashed. But power is more complicated than this. For example, banks are economically very powerful: if you owe your bank £1,000 they will retrieve it from you without any problem. But if you owe them £1 million, and cannot pay, then the problem is the bank's. They can make you bankrupt but they cannot necessarily get their money back. There have been mediations where the threat of going into bankruptcy has been used as a powerful weapon by an otherwise powerless client.

POWER AND CAPABILITY

Power is always relative, and it is always situation-specific: the reason for measuring it at its point of impact rather than its source. Too often power is measured in terms of its potential rather than its actual value. This is why it is useful to measure *capability* as well as power; it takes into account all the factors which expand or limit the effectiveness of power. It is also a useful antidote to people's tendency either to overestimate their own power, and underestimate that of their opponents; or the reverse, to become trapped in the mentality of the victim. Power is also relative to the time available to use it. The closer a situation gets to one side's deadline for agreement, the more power the other side has.

For me, the best example of the difference between power and capability was the TWA hijack in Beirut in the summer of 1985, when a few Lebanese with pistols had the capability to hold the United States to ransom. The immense power of the Sixth Fleet in the Mediterranean, complete with aircraft carriers, cruise missiles and every instrument of modern warfare, was useless because it was inappropriate to the situation.

A final aspect of power and capability which was touched on in the last chapter and deserves further mention is that of *legitimacy*. Most people have a powerful need to feel legitimate because it underpins their sense of personal identity and integrity, and to this extent considerations of legitimacy are for some negotiators a constraint on the use of power. But beware of projecting your own sense of legitimacy on to others: they may not share it. To take an extreme example, dictators use tactics to ensure survival which are anathema to the presidents or prime ministers of democracies. For the dictator, the need to survive determines what is legitimate. Failure to appreciate this fully regularly results in good democrats being shocked at the dictator's wickedness.

THE STRUGGLE FOR POWER AND CONTROL

We often talk rather blithely about 'power struggles' without reflecting very deeply on what it really means to struggle for power. What is really going on when people turn an argument into a power struggle? What is so seductive about the need to win? How can mediation turn a power struggle into something more useful? The answers here are necessarily tentative, but they go to the heart of what we are trying to do in mediation.

It is useful to think of power struggles simply as an extreme form of any relationship between two human beings or groups of human beings. Every interaction between people provides an opportunity for someone to take something out of the interaction. Most of the time this 'something' is probably routine or mundane. For example, if you go to a shop, one product of your interaction with the shopkeeper is the article you buy. But every interaction also involves 'invisible products'. Your quick gossip with the shopkeeper may be pleasant for both of you by affirming a sense of community. Likewise, if you play a game with your child, one of the invisible products is a strengthening of the relationship, another is the feeling of love you may both get.

Power struggles may ostensibly be about land, or property, or money: but they are also about the invisible products. These may be the need for a feeling of dominance, the need for the self-esteem which comes from being assertive, the need to feel the thrill of exerting power, regardless of what it achieves. There is no such thing as a 'senseless' power struggle. Enjoying power is about enjoying the *sensation* of power, the seductive feeling of *being in control.* You may remember a recent advertisement for gas whose tag was 'Don't you just love being in control?' accompanied by pictures of celebrities flicking their thumbs to produce a blue flame. Obviously someone had done some market research and discovered that what consumers wanted was a feeling of being in control – even if it was just to be captain of their own cooker.

You can see the effects of this struggle for control everywhere. People get married out of love and unmarried when they fail to control each other; business partnerships happen when people link up to pool their energies and talents, and fail because the partners then fight over who controls them. Parents seek to control their children, and in doing so turn them into rebels and misfits. Governments, even those committed to 'power for the people', tend to centralize and suppress those same people, because ultimately to be in power but not in control does not make sense.

Being in control is not, of itself, a bad thing but the problem is that being in control of one's own destiny is not enough for some people. For them, being in control means, by definition, being in control of others: it is essential to their wellbeing. The trouble is, controlling others may make you feel good, and powerful, but it has the opposite effect on those you control. However good the intentions of the person doing the controlling – whether the over-protective parent or the benevolent despot – people will always find ways to resist that control: and so the power struggle will ensue.

Now, how do you break out of this cycle of using power in order to control, and the resistance to control which leads others to use their power in return? The short answer is that people have to find their sense of being powerful and in control from other sources. The job of the mediator is to help them find those other sources of control, and in doing so wean them from the power struggle. And *wean* is the operative word, because the need for control is an addiction like any other. The reluctance of some people to give up the quest for control, to give up the old hierarchies, and therefore to give up the struggle for power, testifies both to the power of this addiction and the 'cold turkey' impact of relinquishing it.

BREAKING OUT OF THE POWER STRUGGLE

Where, then, is the need for control diverted? What does the mediator point you at instead? There are four elements in any situation on to which people can focus, but the mediator's real skill is as much in shaping the nature of that focus as in the directing of it:

> The first shift in focus is *away* from the other people and *on to* themselves.

By giving people plenty of time to talk about themselves, what the situation means to them, and how it affects different parts of them and their lives, the mediator can begin to deal with the problem of *projection,* which I mentioned as an impact of conflict on page 62. Projection is quite common in conflict situations, and it adds immeasurably to the complications of power struggles. There are two reasons for it, both of which are addressed by the mediator focusing people's attention firmly on their own interests and behaviour. First, projection often seems to be an unconscious means of refusing to take responsibility for one's own contribution to a problem. If you can convince yourself that it is all *their fault,* then you do not have to go to all the pain and trouble of changing your behaviour. Second, when people are internally divided about something ('*I am in two minds about this . . .*'), it seems easier to accuse the other side of being the dissenter, than to have to admit that one is not 'single-minded' about something.

> The second shift in focus is *away* from the other people and *on to* the purpose and conduct of the interactions between them.

The purpose of this is to change the nature of the power and control being sought away from power and control *over* the other side to power and control *with* the other side. Like many of the shifts which mediation causes, this is both more subtle and more powerful than at first it looks. It challenges the underlying assumption of the power struggle, which is '*If I can dominate this other person I will have more control over the situation.*' It replaces this with the assumption '*If we can work together on this then we will have twice as much control over the situation.*' The new assumption may be

143

more true in some situations than others: but the basic shift is from the quest for dominance to the quest for synergy.

> The third shift in focus is *away* from the other people's positions and *on to* the issues in dispute, including the needs and interests of both parties in relation to those issues.

Think of the pyramid diagrams in Chapter 4, which show the difference between positions, interests and needs. I make no apology for emphasizing their importance again here, because it does make a dramatic difference to how you approach any conflict. Positional negotiation encourages power struggles because it obscures any common ground there may be; it encourages people seeking control because a position is such an easy target. '*If only I can convince them they are wrong; if only I can destroy that position: I shall win.*' Talking about needs and fears removes any prospect of such an easy 'win'. It forces people to understand that the power struggle may be irrelevant to solving the problem.

> The fourth shift in focus is *away* from the situation as it is, and the power struggle as it is, *on to* the possible outcomes of the situation relative to the capabilities of those involved.

This fourth shift involves the combination of two factors: the understanding of the difference between power and capability, and weighing up the risks. We have already discussed capability as a more reliable measure of the value of power. Coupling the assessment of capability with a firm orientation towards the possible outcomes of a situation, and the risks of achieving them or not, makes this fourth shift in focus extremely powerful.

ASSESSING THE RISKS OF A POWER STRUGGLE

Every negotiation involves risk. Do you go for victory or agreement? Do you accept the offer on the table or reject it and hope the other side will offer more? The bird in the hand or the two in the bush? Risk analysis is a major subject in itself, and calculating risk is a notoriously difficult area even for experts in a particular field. When it comes to negotiation or mediation, the calculation of risk is in essence the calculation of one's own capability relative to that of the other side, allowing for the impact of people or events – such as a judge should the issue proceed to court – over which one has no control.

> The sort of questions mediators use to help their clients to make such assessments are:
> - To what extent are you able to calculate your risks in advance? Do you in fact have sufficient information to make more than a rough guess at the risks involved?
> - If you cannot calculate a risk, should you take it?
> - To what extent can you prepare for the risks you anticipate? Again, if you cannot prepare for them, should you take them?
> - What are the odds on an anticipated risk actually happening? Are they acceptable?
> - What are the consequences if what you are risking does in fact happen? How bad would it be?
> - If the worst happens, what can you do about it?

Such questions rapidly reveal to people that, first, the risks they are taking are probably greater than they have wanted to realize and, secondly, the consequence of getting the calculations wrong may be more serious than they have wanted to admit – even to themselves. One of the mediator's toughest roles is to act as 'Devil's Advocate'. This title is the name given to a person by the Roman Catholic Church to make the case *against* a person being considered for canonization. The Devil's Advocate is charged with finding good reasons why someone should not be regarded as a saint. Needless to say, Devil's Advocates, whether they are assessing the claims for an alleged miracle-worker, or focusing your mind on why you may not win a case as easily as you hoped, are not always popular. If they do the job insensitively, they may even be accused of working for the other side. The mediator's response is that they play Devil's Advocate to both sides.

Lawyers usually do this – but not always. For example, I was recently asked by a lawyer to assess with him the suitability of a case for mediation. My first task in such a situation is to discover what might motivate either or both sides to seek a mediated settlement, and one of my first questions is to ask them whether they think they will win. In this case, when I asked this the lawyer beamed, and said that their barrister estimated they had a very good chance of winning. *'What is a very good chance?'* I asked. *'Oh,'* replied the solicitor, *'at least fifty-fifty.'* So I asked how his client felt about half a million pounds of legal costs on odds equivalent to the toss of a coin. The solicitor looked thoughtful and admitted that he had not thought of it in quite that way . . .

RANKING POSSIBLE RESULTS OF A POWER STRUGGLE

Whenever people have been focused on a power struggle, they need to be helped to think realistically and objectively about the situation. Mediators can do this by asking them to write down all the possible results of a dispute. Ideally this should be done fairly quickly and produce ten or a dozen possible results ranging from the excellent to the disastrous. The box below illustrates what this might look like if done by Mr Smith and his solicitor.

Range of Possible Results
in
Smith vs. Jones Insurance

A medical negligence case in which Mr Smith is claiming £1 million in damages against a National Health Service Trust insured by Jones Insurance, but would accept £250,000 in immediate settlement.

Best Outcome: —
Jones Insurance pays us £1 million immediately.
- We accept immediate payment between £250,000 and £1 million.
- We accept payment of a £250,000 structured settlement over 10 years.
- We go to trial and are awarded (say) £150,000.
- We go to trial and are awarded

£150,000 but Jones Insurance appeals
and we end up with £50,000.
- We go to trial and are awarded
£80,000, but Jones Insurance had paid
£100,000 into court so we have to pay
our costs and end up with £20,000.
- We go to trial, lose and pay costs of
£50,000.
- We go to trial, win, but lose on appeal
and pay costs of £100,000.

Worst outcome: —

We go to trial, lose, appeal and lose
again, and pay costs of
£150,000.

When a reasonably comprehensive range of possible results has
been jotted down, they should then be put in order of likelihood,
taking into account all the arguments, evidence and capabilities
available to both sides. For example, what is the likelihood of Mr
Smith being awarded more than Jones Insurance is prepared to
offer immediately? Would a structured settlement of his claim
over ten years be preferable to taking the risks of going to trial and
being awarded the same in a lump sum? Just how good is the
medical evidence in his favour? What are the chances that the
expert witness retained by Jones Insurance will be more credible
than Mr Smith's? And so on.

Such an exercise forces people to be more objective about the
situation and take seriously arguments they may prefer to
discount; secondly, it helps them to focus on the issues on their
merits; thirdly it helps them to be realistic about the power and
capability of their opponents. Finally, this too has the effect of
reducing the power struggle by showing them the real potential
costs of putting power and control above the need for a realistic
outcome.

LIMITING THE IMPACT OF SUPERIOR POWER

Finally, what do you do if, despite the best efforts of the mediator,
the power struggle reigns supreme and you find yourself in an
inherently weaker position than another party. In absolute terms,

perhaps not very much, but there are six specific strategies you can use to mitigate your weakness and make the best use of whatever influence you do have.

---

1. When you go into the mediation, be absolutely clear about your 'BATNA'.

This handy little acronym first surfaced in Roger Fisher and Bill Ury's famous book *Getting to Yes*, first published in 1981 and probably the best selling book on negotiation ever written. BATNA stands for 'Best Alternative To A Negotiated Agreement'. What it means is that you should never go into a negotiation without knowing exactly what you are going to do if you cannot reach an agreement. If you have an alternative strategy ready and waiting, you are much less likely to be bribed or bludgeoned into agreeing something you shouldn't. Fisher and Ury argue that a BATNA is a much surer form of insurance than a bottom line. If the other side does not have a good BATNA, they may well end up needing you more than you need them. Andrew Fraley, Technical Director of the ADR Group, also talks about the 'WATNA': the Worst Alternative To No Agreement. If you have worked on your BATNA, the chances are that their WATNA is worse than yours.

---

2. You can enhance your own position by taking every opportunity to increase your knowledge of the other side.

The more you know about their interests, their constraints, their fears and needs, the more likely you will be to push the buttons which will work on them. Remember also to make the distinction between power and capability. The other side seems to have everything going for it, but are there areas in which you are more capable than them? What use can you make of that advantage?

> 3. Emphasize to the other side your ability to help them arrive at a good result: a successful mediation requires your co-operation.

This is the power of the judo throw: using the impetus of the other side to help you achieve what you both want. If you can come up with a good solution which meets the needs and interests of them as well as you, then you will have enhanced your reputation in their eyes, improved the relationship, and increased your ability to influence them.

> 4. This last type of power is increased if you can make clear to the other side the commitments which you are willing to make in order to see that the solution works.

Your power of commitment may be affirmative (saying what you will do if they agree), or negative (warning them what you will not be able to do if you cannot agree). Either way, make it clear from the outset that you are absolutely clear about the options open to you, and that you will not flinch from whatever commitment you have to make.

> 5. Your own skills as a negotiator can do something to change the balance of power.

Seek to design and influence the negotiation process so as to make the most of the capability you do have, and stay ahead of the game. One of these skills may well be that of establishing a good working relationship with the other side despite your differences.

> 6. Insist on ground rules which will protect you from outright bullying.

Make sure the mediation is set up in a way that gives you the best chance to influence the other side. Ensure the ground rules establish your right to be heard, and make it clear that if the process is abused, you will choose to leave it. This is dangerous if the other side has nothing to lose by you walking out, but you can never be sure how badly they want the mediation to be successful.

The ground rules are one instrument the mediator can use to help to balance power when the imbalance of power is impeding the chance of a good settlement. Mediators usually receive some training in techniques for power-balancing, so if you are feeling bullied, suggest to the mediator that he or she take the opportunity to practise them.

★ ★ ★

Many disputes, especially legal and commercial ones, are referred to mediation because there is a rough balance of power, and neither side can be sure of winning if the case goes to trial. Despite this, there will usually be some muscle-flexing during the mediation as both sides try to impress upon each other the strength of their arguments and their willingness to fight if necessary. There comes a point, though, when the futility of this becomes apparent. This is when the mediation turns from sparring back and forth to a joint endeavour, in which the chief weapon is creativity.

Chapter 12

Stage 7: Getting Creative

A few years ago a complex commercial dispute was mediated just before it was due to spend several weeks in the High Court. A supplier of specialist tiles had despatched them to a customer halfway around the world. Unfortunately, these delicate tiles had been unloaded from an aircraft and then left on the runway in the tropical sun long enough for them to be damaged. The dispute was over who was liable for the condition in which they finally reached the customer, and whether the supplier should be paid for the tiles.

It was the sort of case which makes lawyers rather excited, because there was plenty of room for expert witnesses to disagree about the precise behaviour of such tiles in the heat, and there was sufficient vagueness in the original contract between supplier and customer to keep them all happily and expensively in court for several weeks. The expectation was that one or the other would win, and the loser would pay an appropriate sum of money to the other. When the case came to mediation, it became clear that at trial it could go either way. Neither side could be sure of winning – and neither could afford to lose.

The mediated agreement, reached after several hours of mediation and a roller-coaster ride lurching between success and failure, said relatively little about money. Instead, it recognized that the supplier could do with more lucrative contracts in hot climates for his specialist tiles, and in addition could benefit from consultancy work advising on the use of them in more buildings. Meanwhile the customer could earn some useful commission by acting as an outlet for the supplier and recommending his product to other customers. The final agreement bore little resemblance to the expectations either side had on the first day of mediation, but for both the final jigsaw offered new opportunities and was better than going to court and risking bankruptcy.

THE NEED FOR CREATIVITY

Mediation is a creative process. You could argue that the previous six stages have been about clearing away all the obstacles which prevent the disputants being creative. Angry and power-struggling people are not creative. They lock into one solution – *their* solution – which they are adamant will end the dispute. If they are locked into the old adversarial assumption, they will be thinking that the way to get agreement with someone is to force them into a corner. The problem with this is that people forced into corners have very few choices, and their inclination is to fight back rather than to be creative.

If you want someone to be creative, you need to give them some space and increase rather than decrease the range of options open to them. The more problem-solving options there are, the more likely it is that, singly or in combination, they will provide a solution acceptable to both sides. As someone once said to me, *one* choice is no choice; *two* choices merely give you a dilemma; only when you have *three* or more do you feel you really have a choice.

CREATIVE PROBLEM-SOLVING

Mediation makes it safe for people to be creative. The safer people feel, the more likely they are to think creatively and come up with those options. The mediator's job is to provide for you the opportunity and the safety to be creative. What responsibility does a mediator have for actually coming up with solutions to a dispute? You will find that different mediators have different ideas about how much they should become involved in the process of generating problem-solving options. On the whole, I believe mediators should run the process and leave the parties to do the hard work of coming up with new ideas.

Some mediators will push you more than others, perhaps asking questions to get you to pursue another angle, or using the techniques described below to get you going again. Some may even make actual suggestions if you are really stuck, though that should be a last resort because it risks their impartiality.

AMPLIFYING EXISTING IDEAS

It is very rare that people have no ideas at all for how a situation should be resolved. More usually each side has a number of ideas, each of which is unacceptable to the other. It can be worth looking afresh at these ideas and using one or more of the following ways to work through them:

> 1. It is always worth checking that each side has a full understanding of what is on offer.

Sometimes good ideas are rushed out in a shorthand form which can cause all sorts of misunderstandings, so take a moment to review solutions which have already been mentioned and discover what specifically is unacceptable about each. The 'specifically' is vital. For example, a sum of money is being rejected. Check whether it is because the sum is too small, or because the person offering it said it might not be possible to pay it immediately.

> 2. List the ideas you have produced so far and break each down into its component parts.

This can sometimes reveal that although an idea is not acceptable in its present form, with some small adjustment – or combined with a part of another idea – it could become so.

> 3. Take each idea in turn and ask what else would have to happen for that idea to become acceptable.

The point of this is that the rejection of an idea may be caused not by the idea itself, but by the context in which it is being offered. So, for example, an offer of money is rejected. You ask what else would have to happen to make it acceptable, and the reply comes that the money is worthless unless accompanied by an apology. It is surprising how often people forget to mention what they really want.

> 4. *'What if . . . ?'* questions asked about ideas can generate fresh thinking on particular issues.

For example, *'What if one of you spent more money on this idea? What extra resources would that free up? What if that idea was delayed for a year . . . ?'*

GENERATING NEW IDEAS

As I have said, the more potential solutions there are on the table, the easier it is to find one or more which will work. While the bargaining approach to negotiation encourages people to dig into the single solution which suits them, the problem-solving approach tends to be more creative:

— What options are there for creating the outcome you want?
— What options are there for 'mutual gain' — for everyone to get as much as possible of what they want?
— How else could we do it?
— What else might work?

People who feel threatened by the dangers of coming off worst in a negotiation tend to want to stay on safe ground: anxiety inhibits creativity. It may be necessary to set aside some time specifically for a 'brainstorming' exercise. Of all the idea-generating processes, brainstorming is probably the most common and familiar. There are several methods of brainstorming: if in doubt, use the simplest.

> 1. Set a time limit: 5–10 minutes is usually enough;
> 2. Have plenty of blank paper available, ideally on flip charts or on a large wall;
> 3. Suggest a general and open question, such as *'What can we do here?'*

4. Write down every response, regardless of what it is or the form it comes in, and do not allow any discussion or criticism of ideas while the brainstorm is in progress.
5. When the ideas have stopped coming, take each in turn and examine how — thinking as laterally as possible — it might become, or be developed into, part of an overall solution:
   - How would this suit your interests/needs/concerns/principles?
   - How could we adjust this idea so that it is more acceptable to all of us?
   - What else could we do, in addition to this option, which would make the overall package more acceptable?
   - Can any of these options be combined to suit all of us?
   - What has to happen first for this option to become acceptable?
   - If this option were to be accepted, what would have to happen as a consequence?
   - What if we do this . . . ? What if . . . ? What if . . . ?

It is time-consuming, exhausting, and those who have never worked like this will at first find it superfluous, so persevere. There is also a useful side-effect of brainstorming. If, at the end, there is genuinely no option which has not been considered, the inability to find any alternative will help people to be realistic about the options which *are* open to them.

My favourite brainstorming moment occurred during complex discussions over a political problem. (One of the burdens of writing about mediation is that sometimes it is not possible to identify a specific situation.) I was working with another mediator to get two extremely hostile parties to think more creatively about how they might find a way out of their respective corners. We were getting absolutely nowhere, so we proposed a brainstorm. After much muttering about the uselessness of it ('*We've done it before . . . it's no use: there are no more ideas . . .*' etc.) they finally agreed. With much prompting from us, a list of possibilities was produced.

They then spent some time demolishing each one in turn, our gloom increasing as they neared the end of the list. When they had reached the end, and were looking rather smug about the impossibility of progress, one of the other people around the table suddenly chipped in. This was an official from a government not directly involved in the situation, who had said little until then. Very casually he said: *'That last idea. It's no good as it is because obviously neither of you can do it. But what if my government did it? Would you be able to respond positively. . . ?'* And they were off. An hour later, having used the options-testing questions above, we had an intricately designed package of ideas on the table, and the two previously hostile representatives had worked together to make them as realistic as possible.

The mistake most people make in trying to resolve conflict, and the error enshrined so often in the processes of both law and government, is to assume that the bounds of any situation are set in concrete. They need not be – as both the example above and the earlier 'tiles' example make abundantly clear. Most people assume the pie is fixed, that it is a set size, that it can only be cut certain ways, that the choice of filling has to be as Mrs Beeton dictated in her famous cookbook. Yet, as every creative cook knows, there are moments when you have to abandon the recipe.

> Resolving conflict needs the willingness to think creatively, and the provision of a safe environment in which to do so.

JOINT FACT-FINDING

As I hope has become clear, mediation, unlike the law, tends not to believe that the solution to a dispute lies only in establishing the facts of a situation. Of course the facts are important, but when it comes to getting an agreement, the perception and interpretation of those facts tends to be even more important. In an adversarial dispute resolution process, each side engages experts who often disagree about the facts, and people are beginning to talk about 'adversarial science' as a problem in itself. This is a particular problem in environmental mediation, where often the nature of the problem, its causes and the potential solutions are all disputed.

The way around this polarization of the available information is for those in dispute to agree, first, what facts are disputed and, second, what further information or enquiries might help to resolve what is disputed. This can be done by setting up a joint fact-finding process, in which independent technical experts and policy-makers join those in the frontline of the dispute to establish a common dialogue. The technical people ensure that technical information is understood by the others; the policy-makers explain the policy implications of the information available; and the other participants feed back the impact of the information on their interests and concerns. In complex situations such processes have to designed and run by professional process consultants to ensure that people are not overwhelmed by paper, that the technical information does not obscure other concerns, and that the right information becomes available at the right moment.

This direct dialogue among and between the players gets around the problem of disputed or adversarial information, and it ensures that people understand the implications of the technical information, and the scientists appreciate the problems and issues which their expertise is required to assist. More importantly, from the point of view of finding solutions, joint fact-finding is also a way of generating new thinking about a situation because it adds so dramatically to the overall fund of knowledge, and it means that good ideas are not immediately discredited because they were produced by 'the other side'.

ENVISIONING

People who are locked into difficult problems tend to look backwards to the future: '*If only we could get back to how it was.*' This encourages them to chew over the past and blame each other for what went wrong. The thrust of mediation is always towards the future: not dismissing the past and its significance, but ensuring that the need to understand what has happened in the past does not prevent people keeping one eye on the future.

Envisioning is a process used by mediators to help people look ahead. The idea is that people locked in conflict often find it very difficult to see beyond the next move. Eyes on the ground, they stumble doggedly forward step by step, perhaps becoming cut off from those around them, blind to the opportunities just to one side, unable to see the wood for the trees and eventually unable to tell what direction they are heading in. Envisioning lifts them out of this by getting them to concentrate on the more distant future:

- 'How might this situation look in five years' time?'
- 'How would you *like* it to look?'
- 'Imagine that it is ten years from now. Look back and see how far you have come. Where will you go next?' – and so on.

When people have a firm idea of how they would like things to be in the future, then the mediator can ask: '*What were the steps along the way to where you are now?*' – '*What change enabled you to get from where you were then to where you are now?*' This has to be done carefully. People are reluctant to dream about the ideal when they are living the real. But when it works, envisioning can be a powerful and liberating tool.

NEW PEOPLE

Creating new ideas is all very fine – but creating new people? The notion is ludicrous. Or is it? As I mentioned in Chapter 5, people are always telling me that '*You can't change people.*' In fact, we human beings are extraordinarily adaptable. And to those of you who are thinking to yourselves '*Yes, but it takes time . . .*', I would say that human beings can change pretty fast when they want to. How else could we have people falling in love 'at first sight', or turning into instant heroes in time of war or crisis, or doing something 'quite out of character' because the situation demands it. People change very fast indeed *providing they are motivated to do so*.

People caught in conflict can be motivated and helped to change their behaviour, because finding new ways to behave is another aspect of the need to be creative. The mediator has to be a *catalyst* for new behaviour in the same way as he or she is a catalyst for new ideas. This is probably, as you will readily imagine, the single hardest part of the mediator's job. How *do* you get people to behave differently? What can anyone do about people who seem determined to be 'difficult'? (By which we usually mean they are not doing what *we* think they should.)

The mediator can only do so much. You, as a client – and as one of the people with the ultimate responsibility for resolving the dispute even if you think it is all the other person's – can do much to help the mediator in this role of catalyst. You can begin by trying some of the following ideas.

Fresh Attitudes

First, here are some useful attitudes with which to approach people you find 'difficult'.

---

1. There are no 'difficult people', but limits to our ability to deal with certain individuals. Just as we find certain individuals more difficult than others, so certain other people find us difficult. Everybody is somebody's 'difficult person'.
2. There are no irrational people, but limits to our ability and our desire to understand those who think differently from us. People always act rationally – from their point of view. The further that view is from ours, the harder it is for us to understand their reasoning.
3. People always do the best they can with the personal resources they have (from their up-bringing, education, previous experience, etc.) and within the constraints their map of the world imposes on them. To change what they do, you may have to give them new or different resources, or a new map and understanding of the world.
4. To change the way others behave, sometimes our only tool is our own behaviour. Before we can do anything useful:
   - We have to know how our present behaviour is affecting their behaviour;
   - We have to have some insight into why they are doing what they are doing; and
   - We have to know what we want them to do differently.

   And we have to be able to answer all of these *specifically*; generalities are worse than useless.
5. So we have to be flexible in our own behaviour. If what we are doing is not working, we have to be prepared to do something different, and go on trying different approaches until we find one that works. However difficult an individual is, our first tactic should be to invest time and effort in listening, in trying to understand what makes them tick, and in discovering what they really want of us.

159

6. People change their behaviour when they have a good enough reason to change it, and when it feels safe enough to do so. The real challenge for you and me is to discover what, for each individual, from moment to moment, is 'good enough' and 'safe enough'.

These six points I deliver regularly in workshops and training sessions. The responses range from acceptance to outrage. The two most common questions are: *'Are they true?'* to which I respond: *'I don't know: but it can be useful to believe they are . . .'*; and *'Why the hell should I change* my behaviour *when it is* theirs *which is the problem?'* to which I respond: *'You should only change your behaviour if what you can achieve by changing it is worth more to you than what you have to give up by doing so.'* In other words, if you want to resolve the dispute more than anything, it is probably worth changing your behaviour if that is what it is going to take.

The next question is how we make our choices of behaviour. Most of the time, we are not even aware of making such choices: we simply do what we do in response to internal and external stimuli. I suppose it can be argued that being constantly in command of one's behaviour – making conscious choices about it all the time – shows the peak of maturity and self-control; in which case thank goodness for those who eschew self-control in favour of spontaneity. In ordinary life our behaviour is usually a mixture of the deliberate and the spontaneous, influenced on the one hand by our conscious attempts to achieve certain goals, and on the other by the unconscious influence of our up-bringing, education and experience.

Most people in dispute show a similar mixture of calculation and spontaneity. The problem is that people's behaviour during a dispute can cause it either to escalate or de-escalate: it will make people more opposed to us, or less; more angry, or less angry. Unfortunately, there is no easy formula to apply to behaviour. In the real world it is impossible to say that getting furious and yelling at someone is always wrong. The books may tell you that 'threatening' behaviour is wrong: experience tells you that sometimes a hefty if metaphorical boot up the backside can be therapeutic for both booter and bootee.

This makes it very difficult to offer cogent advice on what to do about someone who is being 'difficult' – despite the number of books and courses which purport to do exactly that. So much depends on the individual concerned, the circumstances, and what you are trying to achieve. This is what makes basic principle number 4. so important. Here it is again:

> To change the way others behave, sometimes our only tool is our own behaviour. Before we can do anything useful:
> – We have to know how our present behaviour is affecting their behaviour;
> – We have to have some insight into why they are doing what they are doing; and
> – We have to know what we want them to do differently.

Once we know these things, we can begin to think about changing our behaviour in such a way that it will influence the other person's. There will be cries of 'manipulation' about this if I do not explain further. Manipulative behaviour is, by dictionary definition, 'unfair': it is behaviour which denies the person manipulated a choice. Much manipulative behaviour is in fact calculated but unconscious, like the child who whines for a sweet from the check-out counter while a harassed parent struggles to pack the shopping. I am not proposing that you should behave in such a way that another person feels coerced into doing what you want. I am proposing that you should behave in a way that enables and invites the other person to respond differently should they care to do so.

Responding to Specific Behaviour Patterns

What sort of behaviour might you want to change, and how could you go about it? I want to outline four particular patterns of behaviour which conflict seems to encourage, and suggest how you might respond to each. Please note that I am *not* attempting here to describe four types of people; to attempt that would be to deny the reality that people are far too complex to be put into any number of boxes. Talking about behaviour rather than people will also I hope make the point that people are always more than their present behaviour.

These four patterns of behaviour are not, of course, the only ones you will encounter, but they are common in disputes and illustrate the idea that you have to respond in different ways to different behaviour. They are not based on any particular research, but on observation, experience and positive feedback from those who have found this approach a useful starting point.

---

1. Bullying

Behaviour: employed by people used to getting their own way.

Characteristics: domineering, insensitive to others, certain that they are right, determined to win.

Suggested response:
1. Get their respect. Stand up to them and make it clear that you will not be pushed around. Do not let them interrupt you or shout you down. Hold your ground and insist on having your say – but be assertive rather than aggressive.
2. Once you have their attention (address them formally and use their name as often as necessary to get it), explain your needs, and demonstrate a firm grasp of theirs.
3. Tell them what you propose and how getting what you want will get them what they want.

2. Blocking

Behaviour: used by people frightened of change or ambivalence, subservient to authority.

Characteristics: unwillingness to listen to new ideas or admit the legitimacy of other people's interests; minds rigid and closed, focused purely on the facts and issues, often on

---

the details of them, and relatively indifferent to human considerations.

Suggested response:

1. Demonstrate your equal command of the issues. Be prepared to go over the situation time and again, using wherever possible their approach and their precise words to describe the history and the general background.

2. Listen carefully to what they have to say, ask them questions so that they can demonstrate their splendid knowledge.

3. Lead them gently forwards by asking them what they think the options are, and introduce your preferred option as a hypothetical solution on which you would value their advice.

3. Posturing
Behaviour:

used by people anxious to impress others, out of either arrogance or insecurity or a combination.

Characteristics: attention-seeking, self-indulgent, theatrical.

Suggested response:

1. Give them the opportunity to indulge themselves, show off, parade their prejudices.

2. Focus their attention by gradually demanding more specific and hard-edged responses to difficult issues. Give them plenty of time to talk, listen, and polish their monstrous egos.

3. Find a way for them to save face by having the bright ideas which converge your interests

with theirs. Make sure any commitments you get are specific.

4. Ducking

Behaviour: used by people who are not sure what they want – but know what they don't want.

Characteristics: apparently purposeless, flashes of passive-aggression such as sarcasm or emotional manipulation; reluctance to respond, indifference to the issues, refusal to consider anything other than one or two particular demands.

Suggested response:

1. Assume there is a reason for the apparent lack of interest in the issues. Go slowly, make the situation as safe as possible, and ask sympathetic questions. Look for internal conflicts: passive behaviour often results from indecision or the incapacity to know which course of action to pursue.

2. Invest time building up a relationship, use 'we' as much as possible, try to discover, gently, what is preventing progress, and work with them to clarify the possible options and the advantages and disadvantages of each.

3. Break the issues down into smaller and smaller chunks, making decisions as painless as possible, and specify what action might be involved after a decision, and the time-frame for it. Your goal here is to get a genuine commitment.

* * *

Nobody can anticipate every form of conflict behaviour, and I would not pretend that isolating these four particular patterns is going to solve all your problems even if they are common ones. The underlying approach is more important. Instead of assuming that some people are just naturally impossible to deal with, take the time to work out what they are up to, and how they might be best approached. This is not always going to work. People who are perceived by others to be 'difficult' have usually become used to being dismissed, or patronized, or otherwise marginalized. A small investment of your time and ingenuity paying close attention to them — attention which will have some novelty value for them — may well be rewarded. Above all, do not give up on the 'people problem': regard helping others to create new behaviour as one of the greatest and most fascinating challenges there is.

Chapter 13

Stage 8: Crafting Proposals and Breaking Deadlocks

By Stage 8 you may have been in the mediation for an hour, a day, a week or longer, depending on the situation and the people. If you have found your way through the power struggle, and managed to be creative, you may be thinking the worst is over. It is not. Just as a mediation begins from the first telephone call to arrange it, so it continues until people have done what has been agreed, perhaps months later.

In the last chapter I said that the first six stages are really a preparation for being creative, by removing the obstacles which prevent people coming up with fresh ideas about solving a problem. The seventh stage is a preparation for the eighth, which is turning good ideas into workable proposals, and the eighth is in turn a preparation for the final stage, which is turning proposals into agreements.

At this last but one stage, the posturing and the power-playing may be largely over, but the real pressure is now on. The mediator will want to keep it on, because it is the pressure which brings people to agreement. Unfortunately, it is also the pressure which leads to brinkmanship and deadlock: the last minute effort by one side, perhaps, to push hard and try to snatch something resembling victory from the jaws of compromise. While doing nothing to stop the parties pressuring each other, the mediator will also be working hard to ensure that each side's proposals are as realistic as possible, that neither side does something which could be construed as bad faith; and that procedural problems do not get in the way of agreement.

MAINTAINING MOMENTUM

The mediator will maintain the momentum towards agreement

by periodically reminding the parties how far they have come, and checking, discreetly, how they feel about the progress made. This may be done separately with each side during private meetings, or by suggesting an open review of progress. The mediator will do four things:

1. Summarize progress to date, perhaps by describing the situation as it was at the outset.
2. List, or get you to list, everything achieved to date. If there have been side agreements along the way they will certainly be chalked up, but the mediator will also want to register the 'invisible products' such as a better understanding of the situation, new perceptions of past actions, more clarity about the interests at stake for each side.
3. The mediator will also want to ask you about the mediation process itself: for example, '*How can we make this process more efficient?*' You might reply that fewer or shorter private meetings would be helpful, or perhaps a short break every hour would help people to maintain their concentration.
4. Finally, the mediator will want to remind you that it is your problem and your process by asking what else you think you should be doing. This is the moment at which some small, overlooked issue may come crawling out of the woodwork. Fine: there is nothing worse than someone 'remembering' another issue just as a hard-won agreement is about to be signed.

CRAFTING PROPOSALS

There is a story about an apprentice asking a famous sculptor what he intended to do with a rough block of stone. '*Why, my boy,*' the sculptor is supposed to have replied, '*can you not see the angel struggling to get out of it?*' This comes to mind so often when the evening news, full of some story about industrial or political negotiations, features a representative making a settlement proposal to the other side via the medium of television, or signalling the willingness to compromise, then accompanying it with a threat. The proposal may be angelic: but it may be smothered at birth by the form and manner of its delivery. To ensure that any proposal you make has the best possible chance of being accepted – if that is what you want – it is essential to be clear about *the decision you are asking the other side to make.*

Proposals are better not made at all than delivered in such a way that they make agreement harder. If a proposal is serious, then it is precious and it deserves the final shaping and polishing which will give it the best possible chance of being accepted. To do anything else with it is a waste.

A properly crafted proposal should:
1. Have a good chance of being accepted;
2. Whether or not it is accepted, at least not damage the relationship;
3. Demonstrate an understanding of the other side's concerns;
4. Demonstrate respect for the other side's intelligence and good faith;
5. Wherever possible represent an advance on previous proposals.

The way to discover how a proposal is likely to be received by the other side is to ask yourself the following sequence of questions:

---

1. How, in general, will this proposal sound to the other side?
2. What specific decision am I asking them to make?
3. How realistic is it, given what I know of their situation and their needs, interests and concerns?
4. Will they be able to sell this proposal to their partner, superior, constituency?
5. If I was in their shoes, would I accept it?
6. So, on balance, should I make this proposal or develop it further?

There are comments to be made here on questions 2 and 4.

Question 2, 'what specific decision am I asking them to make?' is to help you appreciate that the questions they are asking themselves are not necessarily the same as the ones you are asking them. For example, when Jones Insurance offers Mr Smith £100,000 in full and final settlement of his medical negligence claim, Mr Smith is asking himself if he wants to take the money. He is also asking himself: '*Do I give up this case into which I have put my time and energy for five years, which has damaged my wife's health, taken every penny we have, and effectively give up my struggle to prove that my life has been ruined because a doctor could not be bothered to do his job properly? Do I accept this paltry sum without a word of apology or regret from the other side?*'

Let us put aside the question of whether £100,000 is too much or too little, and simply consider this from the point of view of how Jones Insurance can make the most effective possible settlement proposal. Jones Insurance might be well advised to offer that apology – mediation being on a 'without prejudice' basis – and break down their offer into so much for pain and suffering, so much for Mr Smith's time, so much interest and so on, and add an assurance from the hospital that the lessons of his case have now been fully incorporated into hospital guidelines. To do it this way would be to acknowledge the legitimacy of Mr Smith's case, of his suffering, and of his wider concerns, without offering a penny more in actual cash terms.

The reason for using this example stems from training work I did a few years ago with insurance negotiators. Their focus was so firmly on the figures and the bottom line for their company that they seemed to be neglecting the human beings with whom they were negotiating. When asked why they did not give more thought to how they couched their offers, the invariable reply was 'pressure of time'. I used to point out that spending an extra few minutes to ensure a positive response to an offer first time around would in the long run save them time and probably money. My impression is that insurance companies are actually getting much better at realizing that they can dispense the currency of human kindness as well as the paper stuff.

Question 4, 'will they be able to sell this proposal to their partner, superior, constituency?' addresses the 're-entry' problem, as it is sometimes called: a critical factor in the acceptance and rejection of proposals. All negotiators have to bear in mind that those they represent have not been at the negotiations, have not had a chance to have a drink or a walk in the woods with the other side, have not spent hours trying to understand their respective points of view. The proposal they take home has to be defensible. Those who remember watching Shimon Peres in the Israeli Parliament trying to defend the Middle East peace accord signed in Oslo will appreciate this point.

It is not limited to such politically sensitive questions. A colleague recently mediated a case which involved the termination of a commercial lease. There was a generous cash offer on the table, and the people who had rented out the office involved could not understand why their erstwhile tenant did not accept it. The mediator called a private meeting with the tenant, and he finally and rather reluctantly confessed that on leaving home that morning he had promised his wife that he would not accept 'a penny less than x thousand'. The mediator got his permission to explain the reasons for his reluctance to accept what had been offered. The other side thought for a moment, and then suggested he could borrow another of their offices which was to be empty for six months, they would waive the rent, and that would make up the amount he was short. He went home happy.

MAKING PROPOSALS REALISTIC AND PRACTICAL

Now, let us look at the form in which you make a proposal. The first standard to apply is that of reality and practicality: is the proposal actually workable? Ask:

- Will this proposal be acceptable to all those who have to accept it?
- Who will be responsible for making it work?
- What specifically do they have to do?
- By when?
- Who pays what?
- Will it achieve its intended result?
- If there is some uncertainty about the desirability or effectiveness of this proposal, could it be introduced gradually and the effects monitored?

– What do we do if for some reason it does not achieve what it is supposed to, or something arises to prevent it?

You may not want to use all these questions every time you make a proposal: but showing that you have considered the issues they raise will help the other side to appreciate that you are serious. If in any doubt, do not skimp on making proposals practical: law courts the world over are kept busy because people did not specify the answers to those questions before they signed up. Time spent on impractical proposals is not only wasted, it erodes morale and the determination to come up with real solutions. The adoption of a small but eminently practical proposal is preferable to much fiddling with an idea which is wonderful but impractical.

WORDING PROPOSALS

So you have a practical and realistic proposal. Look very carefully at how you word it:

---

1. Frame the proposal in the positive: in terms of what will happen rather than what will not;
2. Start with what you are going to do, then what you hope they might do in return;
3. Do not phrase it in such a way that it sounds as if you are telling the other side what to do;
4. When you have a form of words, say them to yourself. Does it sound more like an *invitation* or a *command*? If you were them, which would you prefer?
5. If you want to combine a stick with a carrot, an objective warning of the consequences of their not accepting a proposal is less likely to cause a walk-out than a direct threat. Again, test it out on yourself, a colleague, or the mediator *before* you deliver it.

The mediator will be happy to help you craft your proposals to make them as effective as possible; this is another point at which the mediator will play Devil's Advocate. Scattering proposals at random is not a good idea; do not be afraid to invest some time in working out how exactly to deliver them to give the best chance of their being accepted. Remember that the object of every proposal should be to get one word from the other side: '*YES*'.

BREAKING DEADLOCKS

Just as an agreement may have to be built from many different pieces of a jigsaw, so deadlocks may have more than a single cause. Here are some of the more common causes of deadlocks, both overt and covert, and some suggestions for how mediators, with the help of the parties, can set about removing them.

COMMON CAUSES OF DEADLOCKS	POSSIBLE REMEDIES
People deadlocks:	
Differences of culture and values	– Acknowledge, list and explore differences – Treat deadlock as common problem
Emotional barriers	– Provide opportunity for ventilation of feelings, having prepared both parties – Test for genuine emotional investment in an unchanging position by asking what would have to happen in order for it to be surrendered
Escalating hostilities	– Clarify needs and interests – Describe situation and ask what should happen next
Personality clashes	– Consider new representatives – Review ground rules – Meet privately to explore source of problems
Representatives perceived to lack legitimacy	– Clarify their authority – Seek new representatives – Strengthen links to colleagues, or constituencies
Unexplained resistance to progress	– Check for unresolved resentment at past action and/or hidden agenda

	– Acknowledge impasse and treat as common problem
Issue deadlocks:	
Issues too daunting	– Reduce issues to progressively smaller chunks
Too much uncertainty	– Seek further information or expert/objective input
Disputed information	– Examine assumptions around responses to existing information
	– Seek agreement on common source of information
	– Agree objective criteria to guide information-gathering and analysis
	– Use joint fact-finding
Complex issues requiring joint solutions	– Break up into cross-party working groups
	– Identify separate issues and brainstorm for possible solutions
Procedural deadlocks:	
Refusal to negotiate	– Ask explicitly about hidden agendas, and scope for compromise
	– Examine scope for splitting differences or 'you split, I choose'
Unrealistic expectations	– Discover what parties originally expected an agreed solution to be and reality-test it with them
	– Review priorities
Positions hardening	– Work jointly on long-term vision of possible solutions
	– Involve more parties
	– Reframe issues
	– Review risks of non-agreement
Outside interference	– Look at impact of possible solutions on outsiders
	– Invite representatives of people previously unrepresented
Loss of momentum	– List agreements to date to balance success against failure

	– Break for evaluation of progress
	– Review pressures and constraints
One party dominates	– Review ground rules
	– Review role of third party
All options unacceptable	– Ask why options are unacceptable and look for narrow solutions to reasons given
	– Review best and worst alternatives to agreement
	– Brainstorm new options and adjustments to existing ones
	– Broaden scope of negotiation to look for potential trade-offs
	– List unacceptable solutions and ask what else would have to change for each of them to become acceptable
	– Suggest binding arbitration

HARD BARGAINING TACTICS

You might think it odd for a book advocating consensual processes to contain a section on hard bargaining – the adversarial alternative. There are two reasons for this. First, people very rarely use entirely consensual approaches, so if they are going to use the tough stuff they should understand the game they are getting into. Second, while mediators, almost by definition, promote consensual approaches, they also acknowledge the reality that people still try hard to get what they want.

If you are up against someone who insists on using adversarial tactics, there are two things you have to do: you need to protect yourself and, if you still believe a more consensual process will give you both the best chance of resolving the dispute, you need to shift the mediation back on to a more co-operative footing. The following ideas may help you with both of these.

1. Know an adversarial opponent as well as you possibly can, and try to calculate the line between their tough and their bluff. If you have to be tough in return, you need to know how far *you* can push *them*.

174

2. If you have to play hard, then be committed. Gather your forces, draw your line in the sand, dig in, wait, and do things in your time – not theirs.

3. Hard bargaining is riskier than problem-solving. Know your BATNA intimately, know the risks you are prepared to take, and stick with them. If you have to take risks, be sure your goal is worth it.

4. If you are going to push hard, do it wholeheartedly. If you do not really believe in your own demands, your behaviour will be incongruent: your darting eyes, raised pitch and sweating palms will betray you.

5. Make sure you control the disclosure or concealment of information. If you have a strong hand, make sure the other side realizes it; if you have weaknesses and your opponent is aware of them, acknowledge them with a shrug. If you can, reframe them to look like strengths.

6. If you suspect you are going to be up against a hard bargainer, write a script in advance and get others to rehearse it with you. It will help you hone your arguments and prepare you for the emotional pressures of the situation.

7. Remember that hard bargaining is always a mixture of temptation and threat. You are saying either '*This is what you will get if you do what I want,*' or '*This is what will happen if you don't.*' Work out whether your opponent is more likely to be motivated by pleasure or pain.

8. Don't be personally nice as a way of making up for being professionally hard. Don't apologize for your demands, don't make jokes, don't be self-deprecating, and don't change your mind when challenged, unless the other side gives you a good reason to do so. If they do, it probably means you are weaning them away from the adversarial game.

9. If your opponent starts shouting, sit it out. When the shouting's over, thank them for making the point, and re-assert your own. Never get angry in return.

10. Silence can be more powerful than any amount of shouting. Silence gives an impression of self-confidence, and it may discomfort the other side more than any verbal parry. It gives them a space to think the worst.

11. If there are 'experts' on both sides, make sure your expert is the best you can get, and that the other side knows it. Then

emphasize your willingness to look for an objective evaluation of the situation.

12. Discover your opponents' deadlines if you can: the closer you get to them, the more anxious they will be. Don't reveal yours if you can avoid it. It pays to take a relaxed approach to your own timing if possible.

13. One way of putting some pressure on them without sacrificing your integrity or the integrity of the mediation is to ask that every discrete part of an agreement be individually approved by your opponent's superior before you will discuss the next. This is known as an 'accrual' strategy, and has the effect of locking the other side into the agreement. They will know it means you can offer progressively worse terms, which gives them an incentive to follow your lead if you then switch to a more conciliatory approach.

14. If you know the other side is desperate to get something from you, link it to whichever concession you need which is hardest for them to make.

15. When you are faced with a hard bargainer, never give anything for nothing. Wherever you can, give process and take substance. So if they want a further meeting on a certain day, try to extract a concession in return for your co-operation.

16. Negatives are never what they seem. 'No', 'never', 'impossible' are best regarded as other ways of saying 'yes, but . . .', 'not now, but . . .', 'not quite that way, but . . .'. Wherever you can, use refusals by the other side as an opportunity to be jointly creative.

17. If they make threats, explain quietly that you never make threats and you never respond to them. Then sit silent and wait for their next move.

18. Watch out for the 'take it or leave it' ploy. If you can afford the risk, call the bluff and make as if to leave: by doing so you take back the initiative. If you cannot take the risk, ignore it or, if the pressure is really on you, suggest an adjournment to 'consider other options'.

19. If the other side is using all the tricks in the book already, giving nothing, demanding every concession, there is one simple remedy: leave. Either they are playing and bluffing, in which case they will come after you; or they are not, in which case the mediation was probably doomed to failure anyway.

The only sure protection in any negotiation or mediation is an impregnable BATNA.

20. Finally, and sometimes hardest of all, stay calm and courteous whatever the other side does. They may first mistake this for weakness, but sooner or later they will either begin to think you have some hidden strength which they should be worried about, or they will become anxious about your monopoly of the moral high ground. Either response may give you the opportunity to move the situation on to a more consensual basis.

★ ★ ★

An agreement which either side feels bullied into is not an agreement. It may settle the immediate dispute, but do nothing to resolve the real causes of it. In the next chapter we look at what constitutes a good agreement, and how to make sure you do not lose an agreement at the last hurdle.

Chapter 14

Stage 9: Making Decisions

There comes a point when every issue and every option has been thoroughly explored, discussed and debated, and the time has come to make some decisions. The options may be clear – and in the process of getting to them you have developed a reasonable working relationship with the other side – but this does not mean that you will both agree when it comes to decision time. Each side still has needs and interests to satisfy, colleagues and constituencies to be persuaded, reputations to keep or make.

Once the various options have been reality-tested, and turned into concrete proposals, it becomes a matter of deciding which to go for – you may have to establish some criteria for making the final decisions:

- Which option covers the most common ground?
- (*if appropriate*) We have agreed an on-going relationship is important. All things being equal, which option will best serve the needs of our relationship?
- What safety-net can we devise so that if a particular option turns out to be less acceptable than we think, we can implement an alternative?
- How can we ensure that the agreement works in practice?
- What contingency plans do we need in case it does not?

In most legal and commercial mediations there will probably have been the trading of settlement offers backwards and forwards between you, and a gradual moving down a funnel towards agreement. In multi-party situations, and sometimes in straight-forward two-party cases, the overall solution often combines a number of separate terms of agreement. If there is any danger that the separate pieces will not work unless they all do, ask:

- How do the pieces fit together?
- What can be done to improve their fit?
- Do they have to be implemented in any particular order?
- Are there any further negotiations needed around any part of the package?

At this stage progress may slow down. You may find yourself reluctant to commit yourself until you have had time to think through the consequences of a decision. In environmental or community mediation it may be possible to suggest a pilot scheme, a period for experiment, or temporary implementation of a decision. In the legal and commercial context people usually want a decision on the spot, and one of the strengths of mediation is that it can achieve exactly that.

It is not unusual, however, for people to want to sleep on a decision overnight, or ask the advice of someone else. For example, after a gruelling matrimonial mediation, which achieved a complex, structured settlement after some nine hours, the solicitor of one of my clients reserved the right to ask counsel's opinion before finally committing his client. Counsel responded with the advice that the agreement was infinitely more subtle and complex than anything which could be achieved through a court of law, and the solicitor would be most unwise to alter a single word of it in case the whole thing fell apart. This actually reinforced the desirability of the agreement.

Mediators understand the difficulties of making decisions in such situations. Getting people to focus on the advantages of agreement and the disadvantages of having to start all over again elsewhere, perhaps achieving worse results, usually helps people to make the decision to agree. It is very rare indeed for the results of a mediated decision-making process to be rejected later. People may feel a kind of 'buyer's remorse' ('Maybe I could have got more'), but they are usually so relieved the whole problem is over that regrets are marginal – and usually disappear entirely when they consider what could have been the consequences of not agreeing.

USING 'OBJECTIVE CRITERIA' TO HELP DECISION-MAKING

Imagine that you are off to buy a second-hand car. You can go to the yard and haggle with the dealer, but it's difficult to know what is a 'fair' price for that battered old heap of rust in the far corner. So you stop by a newsagent on the way and buy a copy of one of those magazines which lists the values of second-hand cars according to their make, age and condition. Armed with this, when the dealer asks twice as much as the wreck should be worth, you can smile sweetly and say: *'OK, I understand that is the asking price. My magazine here says it should be a bit less than that. Could you explain to me what makes it worth more than the price suggested here?'*

Your magazine provides what are known as 'objective criteria', the standards by which people can judge and agree what is 'fair' in a situation. The agreement of objective criteria is, if you like, mediation's substitute for the law – with the advantage that these standards are devised and set by the clients themselves. Why might they be needed? From the outset of most mediations, people will be proposing solutions which primarily suit their own interests. This is inevitable and quite right. Mediation is not supposed to be an exercise in idealism or self-sacrifice, but the pursuit of self-interest by reasonably efficient means. An agreement which does not satisfy the demands of self-interest is unlikely to be much use (though one should remember that for some people self-sacrifice can be a form of self-interest).

Once people have declared their interests and concerns, it can be useful to discuss some general guidelines to determine how the situation should be resolved – before any actual options for resolution are discussed. For example, where there are competing options for agreement, and each one is broadly acceptable but differs in the degree of benefit it offers each side, it may be useful to draw up and agree a list of independent and objective criteria against which each option can be assessed. Now, hard-nosed negotiators are not particularly interested in being fair, and your car dealer, for example, may give you short shrift. But given the choice between not agreeing, or applying some notion of fairness, the latter option may well be attractive, especially if it is the only way of preserving the relationship as well as the agreement. The usual use of objective criteria, therefore, is to introduce the notion of fairness.

In hotly contested situations, getting people to generate standards of fairness may also be a long shortcut to generating actual problem-solving ideas. It can act as an interim process and even a learning one before the much tougher work of coming up with acceptable ideas and making decisions about them. The following questions help to produce ideas of fairness, and may also act as catalysts for the production of ideas to solve the actual problems:

- What generally acceptable criteria would enable us to evaluate each option against the others?
- What criteria could we develop which will enable us to assess each option as impartially as possible?
- How would you like your own option to be assessed?

This last question is a return to the childhood notion of sharing a cake: 'You cut, I choose.' More sophisticated versions of it have been used (notably in complex negotiations such as those concerning the Law of the Sea and sea-bed mining) to allow people either to set the standards, or to make the choice – but not both.

FAIRNESS

I am often asked about the mediator's responsibility for 'fairness'. The short answer is that the agreement is your business, not the mediator's, and you are in the best position to judge what is fair, and what is not. Having said this, mediators are acutely aware that an agreement which is blatantly unfair will probably unravel at some point, or someone will find a way of extricating themselves from it, so while they cannot guarantee fairness, they do ask some searching questions about the sustainability of decisions.

Beyond this, speaking personally, if I was faced with a situation where someone was behaving in a way that flew in the face of all considerations of morality, natural justice and reasonable equity and I was unable, despite my best efforts, to make them see the possible long-term costs of their behaviour, then I would consider withdrawing from the mediation. The informality and freedom which makes mediation so effective and creative can leave it open to abuse. I would rather terminate a mediation than see the whole process brought into disrepute, and I always make this clear in my opening statement.

FORMALIZING AGREEMENT

Let us assume that decisions have been made by people who have the necessary authority to make them and the necessary support to put them into formal language. In legal and commercial mediations people are often legally represented, and the respective lawyers will go into a huddle to hammer out the exact language of agreement. When they have done so, the agreement can be signed and formally typed up later.

That is all very well and simple. What can possibly go wrong at this stage? Quite a lot, actually.

Barriers to Immediate Agreement	Possible remedies
1. You have lost track of what has been agreed.	Ask the mediator periodically to summarize points of agreement.

The mediator should also check the status of what has been agreed: it is all too easy for one person's firm agreement to turn out to be someone else's agreement conditional upon something else being agreed.

2. The final terms of agreement turn out to be beyond the authority of your opposite number.	Ask the mediator to find out whose authority is required, and when it will be available. Discover also what should happen if that authority is not forthcoming.

This happens particularly in insurance cases, where a company negotiator may only be authorized to agree up to a certain figure. Should he or she wish to go beyond it, they might need permission to do so from higher authority. If this cannot be received over the telephone, the other side may become quite restless: after all, they have agreed in good faith. You should also bear in mind that the appeal to higher authority is a well-known negotiating ploy to get the other side to accept less.

3. More information is needed, causing delay.	Get the mediator to check whether the necessary information could be telephoned or faxed. If that is not possible, suggest the mediation is adjourned until it is. Make sure a time and place is agreed for the mediation to be resumed.

Assuming this is not another negotiating ploy, it may be better that the mediation be adjourned until they have that information if the choice is between that and outright failure.

4. Other side states need for legal advice.	If the other side is not legally represented, accept (cheerfully) that it may not be possible to achieve an agreement on the spot, and concentrate on making what you have agreed as attractive as possible.

There is nothing more irritating than to have a so-far-successful mediation fall apart because one side does not have immediate access to legal advice. What is likely to happen is that they will go away and consult their solicitor (who is mightily upset at not being part of the mediation). The solicitor will, with the best motives, advise them against agreement because, not having been part of the process, he or she will tend to advocate the ideal solution in law rather than the acceptable compromise. This is a solicitor's job and besides, solicitors will usually play safe rather than doing anything which could lay them open to a professional negligence charge. Solicitors in such a position can do worse than simply asking the client: *'Will this agreement work for you?'*

In general, where someone not present at the mediation needs to be consulted before an agreement is signed, they will want to know their friend, colleague, client or representative was not being conned. It is quite in order for the mediator to offer to explain how the process of mediation worked. The mediator should not, however, justify the terms of agreement reached. That is something for the parties themselves to do.

6. Insufficient trust to make final commitment.	Make the agreement time-sensitive: each side to prove good faith to the other by certain actions by a certain date.

Lack of trust is a common reason for a mediation to fail at the final hurdle. It may be well disguised (*'There is just too big a gap between us'*) because to declare your lack of trust in someone is very final. Trust is so important that it deserves a closer look.

TRUST

Not all agreements require trust to be made explicit. If you have concluded an insurance settlement with a large insurance company, and they have signed an agreement saying how much they are going to pay you, the likelihood is that they will do so. The agreement between you forms a contract, and they would be in breach of it if they did not pay. This is, if you like, a case of the law taking the place of personal trust. Other agreements can proceed independent of trust. Those who have agreed may not like or trust each other, but recognize that it is in their interests to ensure the agreement works. In this case, self-interest is taking the place of trust.

People cannot be forced to trust each other and if, after much hard work, that personal trust is simply not there, *and the agreement requires it*, then it is probably right and proper that the mediation should fail. Betraying trust is probably worse than not having it in the first place. It may be worth discussing openly how dependent on trust any agreement is, and how that trust can be assured.

Of all the 'invisible products' of mediation, trust is the most precious, and it raises the question of what should happen after the mediation is complete. In one-off legal cases, there may be no further contact or relationship between the parties. One of the virtues of mediation, however, is that it enables people to preserve and continue a relationship if they want to. Indeed the process of conflict and resolution may actually bring them closer together. In such a situation, or where people have had to make long-term commitments to each other, it may be important to maintain the process and its invisible products, especially if it may be some time until it is known that the solutions agreed are working and people are living up to the commitments they have made.

As importantly, if the agreements are informal or advisory, there may come a moment when they need to be linked to formal agreements, or appended to some other process, or ratified by people outside the immediate process. Beyond these immediate and practical concerns, it takes time and effort to reach a good outcome in a complex situation, and it makes sense to value and preserve the process as well as the outcome. Besides, situations change and people change, and you never know when you may need the process again. It may be sufficient to have periodic meetings to review progress, or occasional reunions of the principal players to keep the nucleus alive.

If there are agreements and trust to be maintained, the most important clause in any agreement is the one which stipulates a return to the established negotiation or mediation process before any resort to other means. Trust is something which grows out of processes as well as out of solutions, out of relationships built and tested over a period of time, out of risks shared and commitments honoured. Cheap trust is no trust.

USING A 'SINGLE TEXT' PROCESS

In a situation where each side is reluctant to reach a formal agreement, perhaps because there is a fundamental lack of trust, one of the most effective tactics of a mediator can be to use a 'single text'. This is a way to move people towards agreement when:

— direct negotiation is difficult because people will not meet face to face;

— when it appears impossible to get beyond opening statements and the situation remains deadlocked despite all the efforts described in the last chapter;

— when there is a complex package of agreements on the table which will be difficult to negotiate piecemeal.

A very rough draft text of a possible agreement is drawn up — probably by one of the clients with some help from the mediator — and each side in turn criticizes it in terms of how it does not meet their needs and interests. Criticism is much easier to offer than agreement, especially if there is some hostility, but it is still essential that the temporary and draft nature of the text is fully appreciated by all sides. After each round of criticism, the draft is altered and resubmitted for further criticism. This goes on until no further adjustment can be made. At this point the draft is submitted as the best possible agreement to which everybody must assent if it is to be formally signed and agreed. At this stage, there is a simple decision to make: yes or no. It is risk free, because if anyone says no, the whole text is abandoned and everyone goes back to square one.

The great strength of the single text process is that it avoids the need for unilateral action: the old problem of '*if they do that, then we can do that . . . no, you do it first . . .*' Nobody wants the responsibility, and the risk, of making that first move in case others take advantage of it without offering the reciprocal action which would justify the original initiative. The single text procedure is also an illustration of how creative process design can make the difference between success and failure.

PARTIAL AGREEMENTS

No process can guarantee to satisfy everyone all of the time, and there can come a point when everybody realizes that it is a choice between an agreement to differ and no agreement at all. This is particularly the case in multi-party mediations where the sheer number of people and interests involved makes the achievement of a complete consensus — everyone agreeing everything — almost impossible. In such situations mediators have to ensure that the opinions of the dissenters from the general consensus — however few of them – are registered, taken seriously, and efforts made to make the consensus work for them at every opportunity.

Mediators and consensus–builders have therefore evolved ways to enable people to identify various degrees of consensus so that dissenters can indicate absolutely clearly where they are in relation to their colleagues. Finding some way to measure the extent of consensus achieved means that an agreement to differ need not be a yes–no situation and it may prove possible to shape a final agreement to include the concerns of those who dissented from its previous form.

The degrees of consensus are as follows:

1. Total agreement and genuine consensus: everybody agrees about everything.
2. A small and acceptable degree of reservation among some people about some issues.
3. A larger degree of disagreement: it is still acceptable but there is some discontent and it may increase.
4. Sufficient disagreement for people to want to discuss it and register their concerns, even though they may ultimately agree to go with the majority decision because they trust the wisdom of the others and their sensitivity to the concerns expressed.
5. Sufficient disagreement for a decision on the point to be blocked and for efforts to be made to prevent others accepting it.
6. Little consensus at all and a general feeling that more work is needed before any degree of consensus will be possible.

Those who have worked in groups know how powerful the group sense can be, to the extent that it can make people agree to things they later regret. By asking for an indication of how much people really agree with the group as a whole, the mediator can avoid the situation where people will go along with a group because they want to maintain its unity, rather than because they think it is making good decisions. This problem of 'group-think' can be particularly acute in conflict situations because people put a high priority on maintaining a sense of cohesion and loyalty to their leaders.

★ ★ ★

GOOD RESULTS

At the end of it all, how do you know if you have achieved a good result in your mediation? What criteria do you use to judge the quality of the agreement you have achieved? I suggest it may be worth checking the following ten points. If you can tick off all of them, then you will have done very well indeed.

A good agreement for you is . . .

1. An agreement which is better than any agreement you could have achieved without mediation or by any other means.
2. An agreement which satisfies your needs, meets your interests, and allays your fears, and which does the same for others to the extent necessary to ensure it works.
3. An agreement built around the overall best option or combination of options after consideration of all the possible options.
4. An agreement which has legitimacy for all those party to it, for those they represent, and for an objective observer. In other words, it must be possible for people to regard it as 'fair'.
5. An agreement reached efficiently, cost-effectively, and as amicably as possible in the circumstances.
6. An agreement where the commitments made are realistic, practical, can be adhered to, and can achieve what they are intended to achieve.
7. An agreement which has a pre-designed safety net in case something goes wrong, and includes a commitment from the parties to return to mediation before resorting to adversarial methods.
8. An agreement which improves communications between those involved, builds trust to the extent possible, and contributes directly to improving the

relationship if that is one of the purposes of the agreement.

9. An agreement whose achievement has taught you more about the other people involved, more about yourself, and more about how to negotiate effectively and resolve conflict consensually.

10. An agreement which leaves you and your opposite numbers feeling good about what you have achieved, and positive about the next time.

AFTER THE MEDIATION

It is the end of a long day. You have signed the agreement you have reached, shaken hands with the other side (permitting yourselves a weary and guarded smile), and muttered sternly about looking forward to receiving a formal copy of the final agreement by the first post.

You probably don't thank the mediator (because if the job has been done properly, you will think you did not really need a mediator anyway). More importantly, you do not wink at the mediator, go for a cosy drink with the mediator, or do anything else to arouse even the slightest whisper of suspicion in the other side about your relationship with the mediator.

When you receive your copy of the agreement, check that it reflects absolutely what you agreed. If there is a point you want to change, think long and hard before even suggesting it:

— could it induce the other side to ask for revisions?
— is it worth the risk of the agreement unravelling?
— could it damage the new relationship you have painstakingly constructed with the other side?

The general advice here is not to tamper with an agreement once it has been reached unless and until it actually proves unworkable. If something you have agreed is clearly not going to work in practice, then telephone the other side, ask if they have a similar concern, and suggest a meeting to review the point. At the slightest hint of a problem, ask the other side if they would like to reconvene with the mediator to discuss the point. Although you may think, having achieved the first agreement, that you no longer need a mediator, do not underestimate the chances of your delicate relationship coming unstuck when pressure is put on it. After all, you may find the other side is holding *you* responsible for the agreement not working.

★ ★ ★

The mediation is over. You have made every effort and agreement has finally proved elusive. If the latter, does failure to agree mean the mediation has been a waste of time? Even if you have not agreed, the chances are that you have narrowed the issues and you now have a much better understanding of the dispute and the other side's arguments. You may also find that one of you gets on the telephone tomorrow and suggests it would be a shame to waste all that hard work, and surely with one more heave you will reach agreement. Quite a proportion of mediations do not produce agreement on the day, but do so some days later as a result of the progress made. Mediation is rarely a complete waste of time.

PART THREE:

Where to Find Your Mediator

Chapter 15

Mediation in Legal and Commercial Disputes

Since Alternative Dispute Resolution first began to be widely discussed in the United Kingdom towards the end of the 1980s, a range of organizations have been established to provide it, and some hundreds of people, mainly lawyers, have been trained to act as mediators in legal and commercial disputes. At present the two major ADR providers and training bodies are the Centre for Dispute Resolution (CEDR) and the ADR Group. Various ADR processes, and arbitration, are also offered by the Chartered Institute of Arbitrators, The British Academy of Experts, and the City Disputes Panel.

ADR TRAINING

The training regimes of ADR organizations are broadly similar: a combination of mediation theory, intensive role play and debrief of cases, and modules focusing on specific issues such as communication problems or ethical matters. The training is then followed by a period of 'pupillage', where the trainee mediator first observes a more experienced mediator in action, and then acts as the mediator under the supervision of a tutor. Once the trainee has been exposed to this real-life mediating and the tutor is happy that he or she can cope with the demands, then that person may be accredited and thereafter called upon to mediate in specific disputes.

That, at least, is the theory. In practice, the number of mediators with extensive mediation experience is still relatively limited because there have always been more people wanting to mediate than cases being referred to mediation. As the use of mediation grows in the wake of Lord Woolf's recommendations for the reform of civil litigation, so this unsatisfactory position will gradually rectify itself.

This slow progress has a number of advantages from the consumer's point of view. First, the limited number of cases coming to mediation, and the large number of mediators wanting experience, means that the canny consumer may well be able to get a case mediated for less than the rates being published. Second, the providers are still in the stage of creating a market for mediation, so they need to maintain their success rates at the current 90 per cent plus level. This means that they will assess potential cases for mediation very carefully: they do not want unsuitable cases going to mediation, failing to settle, and upsetting the statistics. Accurate case assessment has always been a priority, but the concern for success means that your case is unlikely to be referred to mediation unless there is a very good chance of mediation succeeding.

CURRENT USAGE

Mediation is the only ADR process being used regularly by business, industry and the professions. The following examples of recent cases reported by CEDR and the ADR Group will give you an idea of how it is being used. The details have been left deliberately vague to preserve the anonymity of those concerned. These cases were all settled in one day except where stated otherwise:

- Multi-million pound international utilities dispute, successfully resolved in a five-day mediation.
- £15,000 construction dispute involving a local authority.
- £140,000 dispute arising out of various office equipment leasing contracts.
- Compensation claim over alleged negligent building work on bungalow. Defendant counter-claim for unpaid invoices.
- £65,000 dispute arising between a design and marketing company and a local authority over the production of marketing literature.
- Four-party construction dispute involving a claim for £2.8

million and a counter-claim for £365,000, successfully resolved in four days.

- Alleged 'passing off' of design for innovative electrical appliance.
- £65,000 professional indemnity dispute involving a lending company and an insurance company.
- Haulage contractor in dispute with carpet manufacturer over delivery rates and expenses.
- £15,000 charities tribunal dispute.
- £500,000 construction dispute already in lengthy arbitration proceedings, successfully mediated in two days.
- Industrialist cancels warehouse contract. Main and sub-contractors suing for loss of profits.
- Retiring senior partner of professional partnership in dispute with his ex-partners following his early retirement.
- Local authority in dispute with its own Direct Labour Organization over supply of additional services.
- Allegations of sexual impropriety in letter, subsequently made public, leading to libel case.
- Farmer suing agricultural contractor over fodder failure.
- Insurance company in dispute with one of its own customers over alleged storm damage to his property.

The resolution of that final case was particularly interesting. The case centred on whether the damage for which compensation was being claimed had been caused by a single storm, as alleged, or was the result of wear and tear over several years. The case had already proved expensive for each side, and both were anxious to resolve it. While mediation was proposed, the ADR Group case administrator did not believe the case would settle without some input on the cause of damage. He therefore appointed a construction engineer to act as a neutral expert in addition to the mediator. They both met on site with the homeowner and the insurer's representative. The expert was called on and in the way of experts said that it was probably 'a bit of this and a bit of that', which brought home to both sides the expense and risks both would incur should the case go to trial. An agreement was reached after a couple of hours of negotiation – and three years of fruitless argument.

Not represented in that list, surprisingly, but becoming

increasingly common are personal injury and medical negligence cases. Partnership disputes are also increasingly popular subjects for mediation because of the personal relationships involved and the information technology industry seems to have discovered ADR: not before time, given that its whole thrust is towards speed and efficiency.

Both CEDR and ADR Group have become involved beyond their original intentions of simply offering mediation to people who need it. CEDR, for example, has run training courses in mediation as far afield as Hong Kong, while ADR Group has devised and implemented a specialist mediation scheme for the Housing Association Tenants Ombudsman Service. Both organizations have also spawned a wealth of ideas designed to advance the provision of mediation generally. CEDR has established three regional centres and a growing reputation in handling large, complex cross-border disputes; recent cases took CEDR mediators to India and Indonesia. ADR Group meanwhile has established two networks of professional firms: ADR Net is a national network of over thirty law firms, each of which has mediators specializing in disputes in particular areas of the law; and ADR Register, a larger network of over 100 firms is designed to help solicitors who want to specialize in representing their clients in mediation.

LOOKING FORWARD

One interesting development has been the arrival of several Dispute Resolution Centres. These are very much *local* initiatives, but supported by ADR Group, and have been established so far in Darlington, Gloucester and Colchester with the aim of providing individuals, smaller companies and statutory bodies with a straightforward and cost-effective means to resolve local disputes. They also provide local solicitors with a service through which they can assist clients who cannot afford to litigate.

Local Dispute Resolution Centres are the brainchild of Andrew Fraley, ADR Group's Technical Director. His vision is that eventually every city and town will have its own dispute resolution centre rather as currently many have their own courts. In the short to medium term, he sees the possibility of these centres being provided and serviced by local Law Societies, ADR firms, or members of ADR networks. In every area an individual, a local Law Society committee or a commercial body would take responsibility for establishing the centre and the principles on which it would operate; provide publicity material and instructions for using it; and oversee its general management and functioning.

Centres would need to be established with the knowledge and support of local private and statutory bodies, professional firms and associations, citizen groups and the community in general. Many in the ADR movement see initiatives such as local dispute resolution centres as the forerunners of the 'multi-door court' where every dispute is assessed in terms of how it can best be resolved, and then referred to mediation, arbitration, litigation or whatever other process seems most appropriate.

COSTS

Individual mediation providers should be contacted for details of their rates. To give you an idea of what is currently being charged, CEDR and ADR Group, for example, quote the following.

CEDR bases its charges on the amount in dispute:
- under £50,000:   £350–450 per party per day
- £50–250,000:   £750
- £250,000 –   £1,000
£1m:
- £1m – £10m: £1,250
- £10m and over: negotiable.

The above figures do not include expenses, nor, in cases over £50,000, an arrangement fee of £500 which is waived if you are a member of CEDR, or reduced to £300 if you are a client of one of their member firms.

ADR Group charges slightly differently:

- From £60–85 per party per hour for 'average' 5–7 hour mediations
- Half-day mediation at £350 per party
- For low-value cases (under £25,000), a 90-minute mediation, on a 'Mediated Settlement Day' during which

a mediator will help resolve several cases, costs £175 per party
- Telephone mediation for smaller cases at £50 per party
- Mediated 'Pre-Litigation Review' sessions, designed to help the parties decide whether to proceed with litigation, are negotiated case-by-case.

Both these organizations run membership schemes for individuals and organizations which may help to reduce costs if you are a regular user, and the same may apply to other providers. They will also establish specialist mediation schemes in collaboration with specific firms or trade bodies, and provide training in mediation. Finally, most providers offer a free case assessment service to help you decide whether your case is appropriate for mediation. As providers admit, a detailed discussion of the case with someone trained in mediation can often provide some valuable insight into what might resolve the case – without it ever going to mediation: which is good news for the consumer and bad luck on the would-be mediator.

CONTACTS

CEDR
100 Fetter Lane, London EC4A 1DD, Tel: 0171 430 1852, Fax: 0171 430 1846

ADR Group
46 Mount St, London W1Y 5RD *and* 36–38 Baldwin St, Bristol BS1 1NR, Freephone: 0800 61 61 30, Fax: 0117 929 4429

British Academy of Experts
116–8 Chancery Lane, London WC2A 1PP, Tel: 0171 637 0333, Fax: 0171 637 1893

Chartered Institute of Arbitrators
24 Angel Gate, City Road, London EC1V 2RS, Tel: 0171 837 4483,   Fax: 0171 837 4185

City Disputes Panel Ltd
5th Floor, 3 London Wall Buildings, London EC2M 5PD, Tel: 0171 638 4775, Fax: 0171 638 4776

OTHER PROVIDERS

The majority of all legal and commercial mediations are carried out under the auspices of CEDR or ADR Group. However, the increasing numbers of trained mediators mean that a number of individuals, singly or in partnership, have established their own mediation practices. The lack of any professional body in the United Kingdom to date means that it is impossible to know who such individuals are, the extent or terms of the services they offer, and the training they have. This poses a problem for a guide such as this because currently anyone can stick up a brass plate and call themselves a mediator.

If you would prefer to use an independent mediation consultant or provider rather than CEDR or ADR Group, I can best advise you to scan the Yellow Pages or visit your local library or Citizens Advice Bureau in search of them. Some are also listed in the directory compiled by Mediation UK (see page 232). At the present time mediation services are usually provided in conjunction with other professional services so it may also be worth ringing local law firms and asking if they have an ADR specialist.

Finally, do bear in mind the points in Chapter 7 when choosing a mediator and, whenever you can, get a recommendation from someone who has used him or her previously.

Chapter 16

Mediation in Separation and Divorce

The figures are frightening. One in three of new British marriages now ends in divorce, and 40 per cent of second marriages. One in six of our children live in one-parent households. Some 150,000 children go through divorce every year, of whom 66 per cent are less than eleven years old, and 25 per cent less than five years old.

Divorce is often cited as the next most stressful life experience after bereavement. In some ways it may even be worse: it is a very public sign of 'failure', which sometimes lingers on for years and even decades beyond the event. It is not even as if divorce is the 'end'. The fall-out goes on: it is evident in the appearance of single parent families well up in the poverty stakes; it is a factor in the background of many young criminals; and for a proportion of children the divorce of their parents can result in poorer psychological health, poorer relationships and lower social and financial status and income. However, research has suggested that *how* conflict between parents is handled can be extremely important. One study (Lunn 1984) showed that parents who cooperated could actually protect and even enhance their children's performance and wellbeing after divorce. In short, anything which can be done to reduce the impact of divorce, especially on children, has to be a good idea.

NEW APPROACHES TO DIVORCE

Of all the uses of mediation, it is perhaps the growing awareness of its potential to reduce the impact and the bitterness of divorce which has most inspired those who believe in it. Somehow the turmoil of a commercial dispute pales into insignificance beside the agonies of a disintegrating family. While we wait to discover

200

how many of Lord Woolf's proposals will be implemented, family mediation is the branch of ADR most likely to be given a formal place as part of our legal system and its dispute resolution procedures, albeit non-mandatory and out of court. In December 1993, the Government's Green Paper 'Looking to the Future: Mediation and the Ground for Divorce', positioned mediation as 'the norm rather than the exception', with legal advice in a supporting rather than determining role. This was followed in April 1995 by the presentation of a White Paper, in which the Lord Chancellor said that his proposals were aimed at reducing the bitterness, hostility and sense of injustice that so often accompanies the breakdown of marriage, in part by removing the adversarial nature of the present laws.

The main points in the White Paper are as follows:

- Divorce available after twelve months for reflection;
- Arrangements for children and finance will have to be settled before a divorce is granted, though courts may in some circumstances grant divorces sooner if it is in the interests of the children;
- Abolition of the need to allege fault to obtain a quick divorce;
- Single ground for divorce will be the 'irretrievable breakdown of marriage';
- Compulsory attendance at an information-giving session for the person initiating the divorce;
- Mediation to be available to all, with state funding for mediation under a system of block contracts to local mediation services;
- Legal aid will be limited to specific legal advice before and after mediation.

The White Paper's proposals for reform would mean the biggest changes since the present divorce laws were enacted in 1969. Until then, the law required proof of a 'matrimonial offence', such as cruelty, adultery, or desertion for three years or more. The Divorce Reform Act of 1969 introduced the idea of the 'no-fault' divorce for those prepared to wait two years if both consented (or five years if one did not), but in practice 75 per cent of couples go for the 'quickie' divorce, introduced in 1973, based on adultery or unreasonable behaviour, which enables people to go their own ways usually after six months. In effect, that means divorce on demand, but it rests on the need for allegations of fault – so that hostility is introduced from the outset even if those involved do not wish it. As the White Paper says: 'The need to cite evidence in support of an alleged fault has the effect of forcing couples to take up hostile positions from the very beginning, which may quickly become entrenched. Allegations alienate and humiliate the respondent to such an extent that the marriage is seemingly irretrievable.'

The proposals in the White Paper have two main thrusts to them. First, they are intended to help save marriages by giving people more time and opportunity to appreciate the consequences of divorce for them and their children, and taking into full account the emotional and financial impacts. This is the function of the 'information-giving sessions', during which couples will also be provided with information about possible lifebelts to marriages in trouble. This reflects the government's concern that Britain has the highest divorce rate in Europe, and this carries with it unknowable costs to the social and economic fabric of the nation.

Secondly, when divorce is inevitable, these proposals are designed to make it less acrimonious by making it less adversarial, and therefore less expensive. Our 150,000 plus divorces a year cost the taxpayer some £332 million in 1993/4, and the hope is that some of this may be reduced by using mediation, and limiting the role of lawyers, though Legal Aid will still be available for advice before and after mediation when couples will need to convert their agreements into a legally-binding court order. Though mediation will not be compulsory, the court would have the power to refer a couple to mediation to discuss whether it would help their situation.

At the time of writing this it was impossible to know exactly what new procedures would be in place by the time of publication. So rather than offer more practical information, which may turn out to be misleading, I am contenting myself with offering three comments on what is proposed in the White Paper. First, while of course I am delighted to see mediation being given such a prominent role, I wonder if there is a danger of it being seen as a kind of universal panacea for the pain of divorce, or even as a branch of family therapy acting as a final safety net for disintegrating marriages? Family mediators have always drawn a firm line between family therapy and family mediation. Family mediation is not family therapy; it is not designed to stick marriages back together, and it is not a means of treating people for the hurt of separation and divorce. In the process of mediation, couples may decide they do not want to divorce after all; or through the mediation they may find it easier to deal with their anger or grief at what has happened. Those are bonuses – the primary purpose of mediation is to reach practical agreements for the division of assets and living arrangements for the future.

The second concern is about the reduced role for lawyers in this brave new world. Divorce remains a legal process, but the proposals here seem to suggest that lawyers will have a limited role in it. For mediation to be effective in resolving all the issues involved in unravelling a marriage, a couple may need legal advice during the mediation, as well as before and after it. Mediation of appropriate cases may be a substitute for adversarial legal proceedings, but it does not remove the need for individuals to be well advised and well protected during the quest for a fair settlement. There has to be the concern that where legal advice is limited, it could place on the mediator or mediators some responsibility to fill the vacuum. Notwithstanding the use of lawyer–mediators in this field, described later, it might be unfortunate for this to be regarded as a new norm.

Finally, if the proposals in the 1995 White paper are eventually enacted, there will need to be a huge expansion of family mediation services. We have to hope that the government will be prepared to support these proposals with both serious money for the selection, training and accreditation of many more family mediators, and for helping lawyers and clients appreciate how to use mediation most effectively.

THE DEVELOPMENT OF FAMILY MEDIATION

It is possible that the proposals in the 1995 White Paper will never be implemented, and for this reason it may be useful for clients to know the current situation. It is impossible to give you this without delving into a little history to see how we have got to where we are, so this section provides some background to the use of mediation in separation and divorce.

The idea of a third party trying to help couples in trouble either to resolve their difficulties or part amicably is not recent. Towards the end of the last century, Police Court Missionaries – what we would now call probation officers – had the task of helping women claim maintenance from or re-establish contact with estranged husbands and wherever possible encourage reconciliation. This role was inherited by the modern Probation Service and casework with families became a major part of probation work in the post-war period. This role was enhanced as divorce court welfare officers, learning from the work pioneered by such bodies as the Tavistock Institute of Marital Studies, began to share ideas with judges and registrars, and this in turn lead to efforts to establish in-court conciliation. (I use *conciliation* and *mediation* in this chapter according to whichever term is normally employed.)

The situation and availability of conciliation through either the Probation Service and divorce court welfare officers or more independent out of court mediation services varies from area to area. In some areas all such work comes under the wing of the Probation Service. It may be confined to the more traditional form of preparing reports for the court, or it may include a specific conciliation service operated by welfare officers. Even in areas where the use of conciliation is limited, however, welfare officers seek to explore and develop all the options for agreeing areas for settlement, and use a generally 'conciliatory' approach in their preparation of reports. Mediation and report-writing cannot be conducted by the same officer in the same case: Practice Directors and Home Office Standards forbid this.

In other areas there is co-operation between an independent service and the divorce court welfare system. Here there is a clear differentiation between the role of welfare officers in co-operation with the judiciary (with their tasks being largely confined to preparing reports and conducting brief settlement attempts at the court) and the efforts of the independent service to work with the parties and their solicitors at the suggestion of, or with the agreement of, the court.

While the Probation Service has been wrestling with the evolution of its role in relation to families and the work of other agencies, the 'independent' mediation (the word 'conciliation' was used until very recently) services have been expanding. The independent family mediation services originated in the failure of successive governments to implement the proposals of the 1973 Finer Report, which included a Family Court with a family conciliation service as an integral part of it. The Finer Report argued that a court battle was about the worst possible way to help people play Happy Divided Families. Since then many people have argued for family mediation as a way of saving public time and money, but the overriding argument has always been that mediation is the best way to deal with the traumas of divorce for the separating couple, and provide some stability for their children.

The lack of official response to the Finer Report prompted a pioneering group of solicitors, counsellors and social workers to set up the first voluntary sector divorce mediation scheme in Bristol in 1978. By 1981 there were twenty such services and the National Family Conciliation Council was formed. There are now over sixty Out of Court Mediation Services affiliated to National Family Mediation, the NFCC's successor, surviving on a mixture of small grants, charitable trusts, and minimal client fees. All are the result of local efforts and local initiatives. National Family Mediation coordinates the work of these services by operating regional support structures and national selection, training and accreditation for all mediators. All services work to a national Code of Practice, agreed jointly with the Family Mediators Association (see below) and the Law Society, in order to co-operate with solicitors advising the couple so that legal battles are avoided so far as possible.

FAMILY MEDIATION IN PRACTICE

Mediation does not aim to make divorce any easier, but it can reduce some of the stresses involved and help the divorcing couple to make sensible decisions about, in particular, the welfare of their children. Until quite recently the future of the children was the main focus. While the Children Act of 1989 reinforces this focus, in practice it can be difficult to separate the future welfare of children from the other aspects of divorce. This has been one of thrusts behind the development of 'comprehensive' or 'all issues' mediation, which began with the founding of the private sector Family Mediators Association in 1988. This is an interdisciplinary association of family solicitors and family counsellors and welfare workers, which argues that most people who wish to divorce have to make decisions about every aspect of their lives together – money, property, and pensions – as well as children. The FMA uses a 'co-mediation' process in which a lawyer mediator is teamed up with a mediator with a background in social work or family therapy. The idea is that this pair of people can bring a wider range of experience and expertise to the mediation than could either working singly, or could two people from a similar professional background.

National Family Mediation services are also increasingly offering all issues mediation, in which legal, tax, welfare rights and other technical expertise is introduced. There are several ways of doing this, for example by using a mediator with legal knowledge or calling on a consultant who remains outside the actual mediation process. One point needs to be underlined in relation to co-mediation and all issues mediation, and in fact in relation to family mediation generally. As in mediation in other contexts, it is not the job of the mediators to advise a divorcing couple on the disposal of their assets or the custody of their children. The mediators' job is to help the couple negotiate their own arrangements in the light of what they learn and experience during the mediation.

Unlike most commercial mediation, about 40% of family mediations involve more than one session. Resolving issues relating to children, mainly custody and access, requires an average of 1–3 sessions, while resolving all issues requires 4–8 depending on their complexity. As with all mediation, our understanding of using it, of which processes are best for which type of situation, is still developing. It is more than possible that in future different types of mediation process may be used to deal with different issues, so these figures may change. The published success rates are somewhat lower than legal and commercial mediation. In 1992 NFM reported that in 38% of cases all the issues had been settled, while some issues were settled in 34% and there was at least a reduction in tension in another 12%. Such figures should not, however, be taken too literally. Definitions of 'success' in this field are notoriously variable, and the figures do not always differentiate between 'all issues' and 'children only' mediation.

PREPARING FOR FAMILY MEDIATION

There are a number of factors to bear in mind when it comes to deciding whether mediation is the correct option should you be so unfortunate as to be going through a divorce. First, it is essential to be clear what issues you want to be mediated and to choose the mediators best suited to that job. Discuss with them whether you intend to mediate all the issues, or just those involving your children.

Second, take plenty of time to study the information you are sent prior to the mediation. National Family Mediation, for example, is currently developing a pack of information which includes a series of forms to help you gather all the information which will be required during the mediation. If you are unclear about any of the information you receive, do ask the mediating body for help and advice: that is what they are there for. If you already have a solicitor, you should certainly talk to him or her about using mediation, but do be aware that some solicitors are more sympathetic to the idea, and more knowledgeable about it, than others. If your solicitor seems inclined to dismiss the idea, ask about his or her experience of mediation, and be prepared to seek a second opinion if you think they are not in a position to help you.

While Part 2 of this book describes a general mediation process, and much of it is relevant also to family mediation, there may be significant differences between this and how your local family mediation service operates. Whatever those differences, however, I would suggest that before the mediation it is worth taking plenty of time to think about the sort of agreements which you might want to reach. (In fact, NFM is now producing sample 'parenting agreements' which provide models to help you decide which of you should do what with your children in the future.) In relation to children for example, the sort of questions to think about are:

1. How much time should children spend with each parent? How should their time be structured during an average week? What arrangements should be made for special occasions?
2. How should financial support for each child be arranged?
3. How should children be transported from one home to another?
4. With which other adults and children should the children associate when with each parent?
5. How and how often should children communicate with the parent with whom they are not living?
6. How and how often should a parent communicate with absent children?
7. How should estranged parents manage their future

      communication and relationship in regard to the children?

8. How should their children's changing needs be reviewed?
9. How flexible should practical arrangements be?
10. What should each parent do if he or she thinks the parenting agreement has been broken, or is otherwise upset by the other parent or by a child's attitude or behaviour?

This is no more than good preparation, but in the heat and emotion of divorce it is more likely than ever that the practicalities of life in the future could fall between the cracks. The high percentage of parents, usually fathers, who lose touch with their children within a year or two of a divorce, especially when resolved by traditional means, underlines the importance of arrangements which are both fair and practical.

FINDING A MEDIATOR

The principle bodies in the field are National Family Mediation, the Family Mediators Association, and Family Mediation Scotland (where family law is different). The difference between NFM and the FMA is that NFM still has its main focus on children issues, though its affiliated services, as mentioned above, are increasingly offering all issues mediation, while the FMA offers comprehensive, all issues mediation in every case.

COSTS

The other major difference is in the charges to those who wish to use them. Generally mediation through the private sector FMA will cost more than the NFM services, which are funded from charitable trusts, Local Authorities and by partnership with the Probation Service. NFM services charge a small fee – up to £25 per session – to those not on Legal Aid, and depending on ability to pay, but in principle will see anyone whether or not they can afford it. The FMA charges vary locally, but £60 per person per hour for both mediators is a guide price.

CONTACTS

These are the principle contact numbers through which to contact all family mediators in the United Kingdom.

National Family Mediation
9 Tavistock Place, London WC1H 9SN, Tel: 0171 383 5993, Fax: 0171 383 5994

Family Mediators Association
PO Box 2028. Hove, E. Sussex, BN3 3HU, Tel/Fax: 01273 747 750

Family Mediation Scotland
127 Rose St, South Lane, Edinburgh EH2 4BB, Tel: 0131 220 1610

For related advice and support:

Solicitors Family Law Association
P O Box 302, Keston, Kent BR2 6EZ

National Council for One Parent Families
255 Kentish Town Road, London NW5 2LX, Tel: 0171 267 1361

RELATE Marriage Guidance
Herbert Grey College, Little Church St, Rugby, CV21 3AP, Tel: 017885 73241

Note: *The family mediation scene is changing rapidly, and there are also significant differences between services in different areas. Check with your local Citizens Advice Bureau, Court Welfare Service or solicitor to discover what is currently on offer in your area.*

Chapter 17

Mediation in Public Disputes

Mediation as used in complex, multi-party public disputes goes under a number of names: *consensus-building* is one of the more common. You may even find a completely different term, such as *community participation* or *community problem-solving*, being used to describe broadly similar processes. This reflects both the novelty of the idea and the struggle of different practitioners to make *their* term the standard. My own partiality is for *consensus-building* to distinguish this type of mediation from the two-party model used in legal, commercial or neighbour disputes as illustrated in Part Two. This chapter describes the idea of consensus-building but makes no attempt to describe the process in this limited space.

CONSENSUS-BUILDING

Whatever it is called, this is essentially the use of independent third parties to bring people together and use mediation techniques to help solve common problems. Consensus-building springs from the perception of government officials, business people, academics and others that using adversarial systems to resolve public disputes can be just as flawed as using litigation to resolve private disputes. Nowhere is this more true than in the environmental and public policy fields, and it is significant that the movement for change is being joined by a growing number of those at the sharp end: developers, planners, conservationists, local authority officials charged with implementing, for example, sustainable transport policies, and central government officials caught between government policy and the increasingly vocal campaigning and lobbying groups.

There are also underlying concerns among thoughtful people.

Protests such as Twyford Down, Oxleas Wood, and numerous less well known incidents of peaceful and not-so-peaceful opposition to public policy, have demonstrated the real danger that the law as an implement of administrative decision-making will come into disrepute. Increasing numbers of people feel that neither our political nor our legal institutions can be regarded as reliable or effective channels through which their points of view can be expressed.

The use of mediation to rectify these concerns is still in its infancy in the United Kingdom. In other countries, notably the United States, Canada and Australia, consensus-building has become a fairly routine approach to public policy issues. This is not to say that it is uncontroversial. There are genuine concerns about accountability, for example, and the relationship of consensus-building to the democratic process. Nor is it always successful, of course, but the failures as well as many significant successes have contributed to the learning process, and a whole new technology for reaching public agreement is the result.

REASONS FOR USING CONSENSUS-BUILDING

Discussion with environmentalists, business people and some enlightened officials has identified several reasons for using consensus-building in this country. First, our present planning, resource allocation, and policy-making procedures do not always meet the needs of the people who take part in them; of those upon whom they impact; or of the environment as a whole – or indeed of the planners and policy-makers themselves. Consensus-building enables all those with a stake in the outcome to have a significant say in what that outcome should be, and helps make the outcomes practical for those responsible for implementing them.

Second, current procedures often produce compromises – some of which would be inevitable even with consensus-building – but they are not always good compromises, and are without the 'invisible products', such as mutual understanding, which come with a more consensual approach. Agreement tends either to be dictated by the most powerful party, or to be reduced to the lowest common denominator upon which everyone can agree.

Third, there is an increasing recognition of the need for a move from raising awareness of environmental problems to finding solutions to them. This has been recognized at all levels, from the

United Nations Conference on Environment and Development (UNCED), through the UK Sustainable Development Round Table right down to individual local authorities implementing Local Agenda 21, the local version of the famous Rio conference on the environment. Consequently many more people involved in environmental matters will need to develop their understanding of consensus-building processes.

Fourth, these same people are concerned about the environment both locally and generally, but feel unable to influence either decisions or how they are taken, and consequently feel little commitment to whatever solutions are being proposed. This can be as true of multinational companies as of local campaign groups. We will never be able to raise environmental standards unless we harness the motivation and commitment of those who have to sustain them. Consensus-building offers a powerful and constructive outlet for frustrated energies and abilities. At a time when people are emphasizing inter-dependence, ecology and holistic solutions, there is concern about planning and dispute systems which lead to entrenched positions, polarized attitudes and communal divisions, and which encourage future conflict. Consensus-building encourages people with different perspectives to seek mutual understanding even if they cannot agree, and to work together on common problems even while they are advocating different solutions.

While consensus-building is particularly useful in the field of planning and public policy, and for dealing with complex environmental situations, these are the beginning rather than the end of its value. It is an effective way to teach people at all levels of society how to reach agreement in multi-party situations and can be used among and within government departments, local authorities, organizations, communities, schools, factories, hospitals: in any situation where large numbers of people need to carry forward important decisions. Its main aim is still to provide a decision-making process, but it can also be an effective way of informing, advising and assisting those who have vital decisions to make.

CONSENSUS-BUILDING IN THE UNITED KINGDOM

Consensus-building as part of the wider ADR movement has

been pioneered in the United Kingdom by Environmental Resolve, an undertaking of the Environment Council. The Council is a respected non-government body established in the 1970s to provide an independent forum within which business, government and environmentalists can discuss their different perceptions of common problems. Starting from scratch in 1991, Environmental Resolve has run a mixture of short consensus-building workshops for people working in particular sectors, such as transport and tourism; and a series of skills workshops which have attracted potential mediators and facilitators. This policy has been extremely successful: both sets of workshops have been consistently well attended, and from them Resolve has received requests from specific organizations and local and national government departments for training and consultancy. There have also been many requests from individuals who recognize the future potential of the field and wish to train in it, as a result of which Resolve also runs an intensive six-day sandwich course in environmental mediation skills.

USING CONSENSUS-BUILDING

When I first began to research the use of consensus-building in North America, someone said to me, very firmly, that consensus-building is best used to determine *how* rather than *whether* something should happen. This person was concerned that any process involving only the stakeholders could undermine the safeguarding of public interests and the democratic process. In other words, the decision about *whether* to build an out of town shopping centre can have such mammoth implications for a large area and a huge number of people that it should be wrapped in legal and democratic safeguards. Consensus-building should only enter the fray when, my American friend argued, the decision has been taken and people start talking about *how* the centre should be designed to reflect the interests of its developers, customers and those whom it affects.

While I respect this concern for the democratic process, and the trust placed in the role of the law and the public authorities appointed to uphold it, neither the conduct of the processes they use, nor the end results they produce, are altogether reassuring. I have heard too many tales of 'consultative processes' whose results seem to have been determined in advance, and of supposedly objective considerations of the facts and figures which seem to have been unduly influenced by vested interests. More to the point, you have only to look around to see the devastation of once-beautiful towns and stretches of countryside to find your faith in such allegedly foolproof processes beginning to wilt.

Whether you take the 'how' rather than 'whether' approach ultimately depends on the faith you have in the existing processes. Before we trample on the traditional territory of those who believe in public inquiries and government-led consultative processes, we should certainly gain more experience of consensus-building in practice, and find out how the British use of it might have to differ from its use in other countries and cultures. The most sensible approach will be to use it in parallel with conventional approaches, or experiment with it in situations where those conventional approaches appear problematic.

APPROPRIATE SITUATIONS FOR CONSENSUS-BUILDING

This brings us to the question of what sort of situations might benefit from a consensus-building approach. If you are a Parish Clerk, a Town Councillor, involved in a campaigning or protest group, or working for a commercial organization, you should think about using consensus-building in any situation which has some or all of the following characteristics:

1. Many parties, many issues

These are the situations in which consensus-building really comes into its own. The more people, organizations and issues involved, the more appropriate consensus-building – and the less likely adversarial methods are to produce good outcomes.

2. Varying moral and political values

The clash of different political or moral beliefs has become starkly obvious in many recent environmental controversies. Where there is no meeting of minds, but clearly passionately held views, people need a process which enables everybody to appreciate, if not always understand or accept, the range of feelings, beliefs and perceptions involved. While full agreement may be elusive, a well-designed process may reveal areas of common ground which an adversarial process would obscure.

3. Absence of agreed information

Adversarial processes often penalize participants who confess the inadequacy of their information, or turn what should be shared factual information into opportunities to win debating points. Consensus-building encourages participants to identify areas of uncertainty and jointly agree how the information necessary for good decisions can be acquired. The joint search for information is preferable to each party seeking its own information to support its own case.

4. Differing organizational cultures

People and organizations from different sectors – for example, the voluntary and commercial – have different ways of doing things, different structures, different styles of internal accountability. All this can produce misunderstandings and accusations of bad faith. Consensus-building gives people time to understand how others are operating.

5. Established procedures inappropriate

Adversarial processes are often used because there appears to be no alternative. Consensus-building processes are always *designed* to fit the problem they are intended to address, and if necessary the first step can be to offer some training to those who need to take part in them. When have 'ordinary' people ever been trained how to participate in a public inquiry?

6. No investment in future relationships

Communities divided by contentious issues need, more than ever, to preserve the relationships which make them a community. Adversarial processes inevitably undermine people's perception of the value or possibility of present or future relationships. Consensus-building is oriented towards the future and the need for sustainable solutions, and therefore invests time and effort in building relationships as well as agreements.

7. Need to prevent future disputes

Consensus-building is also about dispute *prevention*: if people understand the issues and areas of potential dispute, and have established a working relationship, it is more likely that they will be able to anticipate and defuse disputes before they can escalate and cause real problems.

EXAMPLES OF CONSENSUS-BUILDING

Although consensus-building is still fairly new in the United Kingdom, there have already been some striking success stories. For example, a couple of years ago the British Wind Energy Association needed to produce some guidelines for the development of wind farms. It was assumed that environmental groups would support the idea, but this was not the case. Following an intensive period of preparation, a consensus-building process was launched and took approximately six months to arrive at a set of guidelines which everyone could support. These were duly published and met with widespread approval because all those who needed to approve them had been involved in their development.

A similar process has been used to develop a waste disposal strategy for Hampshire. Hampshire's three old incinerators were not meeting new European requirements, so plans needed to be developed for an entirely new waste disposal strategy. As everybody knows, waste management is a very controversial issue and generates enormous resistance among those who feel the waste is going to be dumped on their doorstep. Hampshire used a consensus-building process to build the outlines of a new strategy, appoint three expert advisory panels, and develop recommendations which set the guidelines for companies tendering for the new waste disposal contracts. This approach was so successful that Hampshire has since begun to use a similar strategy to develop its transport policy.

These two examples illustrate the way that this approach can be used to deal with both immediate problems and to prevent future ones by building ownership of the solutions among those who have to make them work. Environmental Resolve also provides independent mediators who specialize in environmental disputes.

CONTACTS

Consensus-building, like most of ADR, is simply systematic and applied common sense, and there have always been people and organizations which have taken such an approach to complex, multi-party problems. Management and process consultancies the world over have used such approaches whenever they have been allowed to do so and the situation has been appropriate. The reason for highlighting the work of Environmental Resolve is that it seems to be the first attempt to promote and publicize the value of consensus-building to the public at large, and to encourage 'ordinary people' to become trained in the skills and techniques it requires.

I have a vested interest in promoting the work of Resolve: I have been involved in it since its inception. I also believe it deserves highlighting because it is a significant ADR initiative. In accordance with the ADR commitment to empowerment, Resolve encourages widespread participation in consensus-building and provides the means for achieving it. This is not a club for experts and consultants, but a conscious and deliberate attempt to help people become engaged in making the decisions which affect their lives.

Environmental Resolve at
The Environment Council, 21 Elizabeth St, London SW1W 9RP, Tel: 0171 824 8411, Fax: 0171 730 9941

Chapter 18

Mediation in the Workplace

So far this book has concentrated on the use of mediation in situations which might otherwise result in a court battle. In this chapter I am going to deviate slightly from this to outline the use of mediation within organizations, among colleagues around the workplace and with customers. Workplace disputes can, of course, end up in court, as can disputes with customers, but the main thrust of this chapter is towards *preventing* disputes ever happening.

Workplace conflict imposes huge hidden costs on organizations. It has been estimated (Daniel Dana, *Organization Development Journal,* Autumn 1984) that some 65 per cent of performance problems among employees stem from poor relationships rather than lack of skill. This in turn leads to most managers spending 25 per cent or more of their time ('A Survey of Managerial Interests with Respect to Conflict', Thomas and Schmidt, *Academy of Management Journal,* June 1976) fire-fighting among colleagues or subordinates: time taken from pursuing the objectives of the organization. Both these figures are quite old, and it is possible that, with the increased pressures of work since these pieces of research were done, even more of us spend our working days trying to deal with disputes.

ADR IN THE WORKPLACE

To date, ADR's only impact on the workplace has been in a small number of cases where employers and employees have fallen out, and preferred to reach private settlements of grievance and unfair dismissal claims. The National Council for Voluntary Organisations has recently, for example, introduced a mediation service for

218

charities, aimed primarily at responding to internal disputes among trustees and staff. There is, in fact, a whole branch of ADR devoted entirely to preventing and resolving conflict problems at work. I am not aware that it has been much used in the United Kingdom as yet, and it is therefore not possible to point you to any particular contacts, but it is being widely used in North America and Australia. I think British managers, in-house lawyers and unions need to be aware of it.

One of the reasons that this branch of ADR has yet to cross the Atlantic is that it labours under the name of *Dispute Systems Design* (DSD). The term stems mainly, so far as it is possible to discover, from a book called *Getting Disputes Resolved: Designing Systems to Cut the Costs of Conflict* first published in 1988 by William Ury, Jeanne Brett and Stephen Goldberg. The purpose of DSD is to initiate *systematic* methods of ensuring that conflict and disputes within organizations or established patterns of relationships are prevented or resolved at the earliest opportunity and as cost-effectively as possible. The key word here is *systematic,* and for this reason from here on I shall use the phrase 'dispute resolution systems' rather than Dispute Systems Design.

DISPUTE RESOLUTION SYSTEMS

The basic idea of a dispute resolution system is that high-cost methods of dispute resolution, such as arbitration and litigation, are replaced whenever possible by lower-cost methods, such as negotiation and mediation. If negotiation does not work, that is the time to bring in a mediator; if mediation also fails, then you try a simplified form of arbitration; if those involved will not agree to that, only then do you start using more complex and expensive measures. The skill comes in designing how the system operates in a specific situation.

This systematic approach can, for example, be applied within an internally divided organization, or in any other situation where conflict regularly disrupts important and on-going relationships between an organization and its regular clients or customers. A dispute resolution system is therefore a useful — one might say essential — tool for organizations working towards a 'total quality' commitment or towards improving customer services. Both goals are dependent to a large extent upon the quality of the relationships among staff. Poor customer care is almost invariably an indication of poor management and poor relationships within the organization. This relationship between internal change and external achievement is not always as clearly recognized as it might be.

WHEN TO CONSIDER A DISPUTE RESOLUTION SYSTEM

The impetus for the design and implementation of a dispute resolution system is usually the result of one or more of the following situations:

- There is no regular and established system for dealing with disputes;
- A crisis within the existing dispute resolution system reveals that it is too costly, too slow, too cumbersome, or people lack confidence in its fairness or effectiveness;
- Many broadly similar disputes are occurring and being dealt with on a piecemeal and therefore expensive basis;
- The nature, volume or intensity of disputes is imposing unacceptable strains on other parts of the organization;
- The organization is in a period of change which involves new relationships and partnerships with considerable benefits for all concerned, but because of this there is also a heightened risk of disputes.

Note that 'organization' includes any regular pattern of repeat relationships, as well as any type of organization. Dispute resolution systems have been implemented in bodies ranging from massive corporations to schools and hospitals.

DESIGNING AND IMPLEMENTING DISPUTE RESOLUTION SYSTEMS

The first thing you need to know is what the current disputes are about. This means doing a comprehensive *conflict audit*: living with the organization until you know precisely which of its functions are giving rise to problems. Most organizations do not respond systematically to disputes because they do not know precisely what disputes are occurring and how they are being managed and resolved. Before any significant work can be done to improve dispute handling it is essential to know:

- What kinds of disputes are involved?
- How many are there?
- Are there particular trigger points or warning signs?
- Who are the parties to these disputes?
- Do these disputes recur?
- What are the current costs of these disputes?
- What processes are currently being used to resolve disputes?

When this basic information is known, more detailed investigation can centre on:

- If there are existing mechanisms through which disputes are supposed to be handled – for example, complaints or grievance procedures, staff or partnership meetings – are they being used? If they are, why are they not functioning properly?
- What is happening when people try to resolve disputes? What are the obstacles to successful negotiation? What happens when negotiations break down?
- Why are some procedures used more than others? How satisfactory are such procedures – and from whose point of view?
- What are the costs of existing procedures? What effect do the various procedures have on present and future relationships?
- How often do the same disputes recur because they are never properly resolved?

A successful dispute resolution system depends heavily on the commitment of those who will use it. To make it work, it is essential that they are fully consulted about both its design and implementation. The people consulted should include at least the following:

- All who will be affected by the new system within the organization;
- All outside the organization who may be involved in it at

some time, notably business partners, customers and potential parties to disputes;
- Any potential third parties, ombudsmen, or regulators;
- Any consumer organizations, lobby groups, or share-holder groups.

The consultation stage is important not only because it supplements the research stage and provides essential intelligence to inform the design stage, but because it will indicate the degree and speed of cultural change required for the workforce to accept the new system, and the likely training requirements. The design of new systems for managing disputes is based on the information gained from the conflict audit, and builds on the strengths while eliminating the weaknesses of existing procedures. There are six basic principles in designing a dispute resolution system:

1. Dispute resolution procedures need to be arranged in a low-to-high cost sequence.
2. Preventing disputes almost always costs less than either winning or resolving them; suppression or appeasement can end up costing more.
3. The most cost-effective of all dispute resolution systems is problem-solving negotiation between those directly concerned at the point of first impact.
4. Each procedure should be exhausted before the next is introduced, and each should allow return to the previous procedure if appropriate.
5. There should be consultation before, monitoring during, and feedback after each use of the system.
6. New systems need motivation, leadership, skills and resources to make them work.

Most dispute resolution systems utilize stages going from the least interventionist to the most interventionist. The least interventionist, direct negotiation at the point of dispute, is also the most informal, and allows the disputants most control over the outcome. The most interventionist, referral to an outside tribunal, arbitrator or judge, is the most expensive, most risky for those who do it, and most damaging to relationships within the organization. The ultimate achievement of every dispute resolution system is to prevent disputes ever happening – because people have learned to anticipate and deal with their causes.

Bear two points in mind should you wish to try this approach. First, there is no 'off-the-shelf' dispute resolution system: each one needs to be designed around the needs of the individual organization and its people. For example, if you need to educate every member of the organization in dispute resolution, you might want to consider peer mediation as one of your stages of intervention. The use of peer mediation in a school, say, might be a good way to reduce bullying. Second, while many organizations will be more than capable of designing their own dispute resolution systems, it can be useful to do it in collaboration with someone from outside who will have a different viewpoint and also may be able to deal with issues which are too sensitive to be handled by an 'insider'. An outsider can also absorb some of the resentment which accompanies any change in the *status quo*.

BEYOND DISPUTE RESOLUTION SYSTEMS: PARTNERING

Dispute prevention is the leading edge of ADR. An example of this is *partnering* which has become increasingly widely used in recent years to cut the costs of conflict in major projects. Partnering, like all the best ADR, is no more than applied common sense. It involves establishing close working relationships between project management teams, partners, contractors, customers and generally anyone else involved before a project even begins, and fostering these relationships in such a way that the difficulties inevitable in any collaborative project do not end up in dispute and disaster.

The important elements in a partnering programme are:

1. The partnering process is prepared and goes into operation as early as possible – as soon as a project is even mooted.
2. There is top level commitment from all concerned at the outset and throughout.
3. Once the key players are decided, a joint workshop is held over several days to build working relationships, establish shared understanding of the project's key

objectives, and identify potential areas of difficulty or dispute before they arise.

4. The workshop identifies 'champions' for the project who will take responsibility for maintaining the partnering process.

5. The formal product of the workshop is a *partnering charter*, produced by collaborative effort. It should cover everything: meeting the project designs; health and safety procedures; agreeing to use ADR should problems arise; agreeing to finish the project ahead of schedule and below estimate if possible.

6. The final element is follow-up meetings and constant monitoring and evaluation so that the lessons and benefits of partnering are continually reinforced, and any problems spotlighted before they escalate.

Some will say that good project management already does this, and that is certainly true. But most project management is less systematic than it might be, and the volume of construction disputes reaching the courts, for example, suggests more can be done in terms of designing disputes out of projects right from their outset. The evidence for its benefits is in the results, as in an example provided by the US Army Corps of Engineers, which is the arm of the American government responsible for many of North America's largest construction projects. This was a construction project involving the replacement of a navigation lock on the Columbia River. It was an extremely complex project with a great deal of risk and uncertainty because of the geology of the site. The outcomes put down to the use of partnering included:

- No outstanding claims or litigation;
- Engineering savings amounting to $1.8 million on a $34 million contract;
- Cost growth of 3.3% compared with typically 10% on most major construction projects;
- Project completed on schedule;
- No time lost due to injuries;
- A two-thirds reduction in letters and case-building paperwork relative to comparable projects.

* * *

What does all this add up to? Why should management processes for handling disputes be included in the ADR repertoire at all? The best answer to both questions is that dispute resolution systems and partnering point to the future of ADR as a whole. They start from the assumption that there are usually good reasons for conflict, discover what they are or might be, and finally design practical strategies for preventing or resolving the problems at the lowest possible cost. It must make sense, and we should hope that partnering becomes part of the ADR scene in the United Kingdom before too long.

CONTACTS

I am not aware of any national bodies established to promote specifically internal dispute resolution systems or partnering. It is a definite gap in ADR provision. The National Council for Voluntary Organisations Dispute Resolution Service can be contacted at
NCVO
Regent's Wharf, 8 All Saints Street, London N1 9RL Tel: 0171 713 6161 Fax: 0171 713 6300

Chapter 19

Mediation in the Community

'Community' is one of those weasel words which has become progressively devalued over the years. Politicians talk glibly about 'care in the community'; the judiciary hands down 'community sentences' to offenders; we talk about living in 'communities' which our ancestors would regard as a travesty of what a community should be.

But all is not lost. Over the last ten years a small number of dedicated people have been quietly reconstructing ideas of what we should mean by community – and using mediation as one vehicle for them. Dotted about our inner city areas, neighbourhood mediation projects have been doing the groundwork for a revolution in how we deal with human conflict at the everyday, street level. At the same time many of them have also been rethinking how we should respond to people who have offended against the laws of our community.

NEIGHBOURHOOD MEDIATION SERVICES

These projects are neither well known to the public at large, nor well funded. They are frequently beset with financial crises, and from time to time one disappears, though others are constantly being born. They do not even deal with a very large number of cases when set against the grim totals of crime and neighbourhood alienation in many parts of the country. Yet, for all this, they are doing work which is essential, and which will one day gain the recognition it deserves. While it would be nice to think that some future Home Secretary might have the vision to recognize the significance of these early communitarian efforts, there is much to be said for keeping them rooted in the communities they serve and dependent upon those communities for their maintenance and support.

In *Access to Justice* (Chapter 18, para 21) Lord Woolf recognizes the contribution these schemes are making. He writes:

> 'These [neighbourhood mediation schemes] have made a considerable contribution to the resolution of disputes, resulting in a significant saving to the court system. Almost without exception the bodies who provide these mediation schemes are underfunded. This is not in the interests of their clients or of the Court Service. I recommend they are funded more appropriately. I would very much hope in any review of legal aid the needs of bodies of this nature would be taken into account. In many situations, they provide the only way in which the citizen can obtain access to justice, and in any event they may offer a better and less confrontational way of dealing with disputes between neighbours, where a continuing relationship is often important.'

Not all these projects are without official support and recognition. Of the eighty or so schemes currently operating, some 15–20 are specifically victim/offender mediation schemes, established under the aegis of local probation areas and/or Victim Support, and 20–30 are based around schools. The logic of these connections is more obvious than it may at first seem. It goes like this: if you teach children how to resolve conflict amicably, you will ultimately strengthen a community's ability to resolve its own conflict, and that in turn will reduce the number of offenders, or at the very least increase the ability of the community to seek suitable reparation from an offender as part of the process of his or her rehabilitation.

The organization which acts as an umbrella body for these schemes is Mediation UK, formerly the Forum for Initiatives in Reparation and Mediation. Mediation UK's aim, to quote its mission statement, is 'to make available conflict resolution skills, including mediation, to every citizen in pursuit of the promotion and protection of human rights'. There is something here beyond the normal rhetoric of such statements. Mediation UK is clear that bringing mediation and conflict resolution skills to every individual should be part of his or her basic education for citizenship in a democracy. To this end the organization serves individuals, organizations and projects involved or interested in constructive approaches to handling conflict. It provides an information and referral service, sponsors training events for volunteers, and crucially, gives practical help to people who want to establish a local mediation service.

The growing number of community mediation services across the country, despite the enormous constraints and frustrations caused by lack of funding, suggests that what began as the hunch of a few pioneering individuals is rapidly becoming established wisdom supported by bodies ranging from the Department of the Environment to the Association of Metropolitan Authorities. This much was acknowledged by Robert Atkins MP, Minister for the Environment and Countryside, at Mediation UK's tenth anniversary celebration when he congratulated them on the 10,000 or so neighbour disputes they have helped to resolve, and added: 'In the area of housing, my own department and colleagues in local authorities see mediation as an increasingly important way to informally tackle a variety of neighbour disputes . . . We will be looking to Mediation UK to promote community mediation services and to provide advice and guidance for their development and long-term financing.'

The carrot for local authorities in mediation schemes is that mediation offers a cost-effective alternative to more formal ways of resolving disputes between neighbours. For example, one community mediation service has estimated that a typical neighbour dispute, involving telephone calls and visits from statutory agencies such as the police, housing departments, environmental health, race relations and community advice centres, can cost the local taxpayers over £1,000 if it is allowed to escalate. Should that dispute result in violence and court proceedings, the costs really begin to mount. The average cost of court proceedings, including the Crown Prosecution Service, and the costs of the court and legal aid, is £4,600 per case. The average cost of a case mediated by volunteer mediators is £200, or £330 if staff mediators are used. So here, as elsewhere, mediation is valuable on purely financial grounds. But the real value goes beyond this because prosecution of a disorderly neighbour, even if successful, does nothing to resolve the original causes of the dispute. Inflamed by the indignity and expenses of appearing in court, the dispute may recur in a more serious form.

MEDIATION IN SCHOOLS

Prevention is here, as elsewhere, another theme of mediation. The ultimate form of prevention is either designing conflict right out of relationships — which is very rarely possible — or ensuring that conflict is resolved as early as possible and before it escalates. Conflict in schools has a way of both reflecting conflict in the community, and of spilling out into that community and drawing in the family and friends of the children involved. Conflict resolution training in schools is also one of the most effective ways of combating the problem of bullying.

Mediation in British schools is still something of a novelty. In North America it is becoming a matter of necessity, because in schools where a proportion of the kids attend school armed and there are metal detectors on the doors, a playground row over a bag of sweets can turn into a tragedy. I am sure I did not meet the only parent whose introduction to the concept of mediation was his child coming home from school with 'mediator' emblazoned on his T-shirt.

Training for European children in peer mediation is lead by ENCORE, the European Network for Conflict Resolution in Education, which has recently received finance from the European Commission to encourage non-governmental organizations in the European Union to build links with the new democracies of Eastern Europe in order to strengthen their burgeoning civil societies. Where conflict is or has been a norm, teaching the tools for resolving it makes fundamental sense.

VICTIM/OFFENDER MEDIATION

This brings us to the use of mediation within the criminal justice system: worthy of many books on its own and something to which it is impossible to do due justice here. At the heart of it, though, is a new understanding of the relationship between crime and punishment, victim and offender, society and those who are brought into conflict with society by the crimes they commit. The traditional assumption is that crime is an offence against the State — which is why we have a *Crown* Prosecution Service; and justice is the establishment of blame and the application of punishment as guided by law and precedent. But this is not the only understanding of the relationships involved here.

In other times and other cultures there have been different approaches. There is the Old Testament concept of *shalom*, for example, which is the idea of putting things right and restoring peace and harmony to relationships which have been damaged. This makes crime not the business of the State, but a matter of conflict between the offender and the victim; not a question of pinning the blame for past actions, but of accepting responsibility for them, and finding ways to discharge the obligations created by the crime and its consequences. This approach has the great merit of making crime and punishment more personal without encouraging the wreaking of revenge or the setting up of vigilantes. It ensures the offender sees the offence not as an abstract action against the anonymous State, but as a wound against another human being. It insists that such wounds cannot be healed by State-imposed punishment, but only by the criminal confronting the consequences of that wound and accepting personal responsibility for the healing of it.

Victim/offender mediation rests on the experience that both victim and offender can benefit from a direct encounter designed to facilitate this healing process. For the victim, this is an opportunity to confront the offender with the impact of the offence: a moment of catharsis, of being able to express all the rage and hate and fury which a crime can cause and which, if not expressed, can lead to illness and despair. For the offender, the impact of such meetings can be very great indeed. For example, research on Leeds Mediation and Reparation Service in 1992 showed that of 69 offenders who met their victims, 78 per cent had no further convictions after twelve months, and 58 per cent had no further convictions after two years. These figures suggest that mediation may have a more profound effect on offenders that many other forms of 'punishment' or 'treatment'.

Mediation within communities and within the criminal justice system is the subject of experimentation in various parts of the world. Australia's Community Justice Centres (CJCs), for example, deal with cases ranging from abuse and harassment to property damage and theft, and the police are authorized to refer disputes to a CJC rather than make arrests or lay charges. The CJCs have state funding and are backed by law (Community Justice Centres Act 1983): another example of the deep commitment of the Australian government to ADR in general and the use of mediation in particular.

Behind these uses of mediation is the acknowledgment that our traditional approaches to crime and punishment are proving inadequate and even counter-productive. The problem with punitive approaches to criminality is that they do not address the needs of the victims, there is no provision for direct reparation from criminal to victim, they do not necessarily confront the criminal with responsibility for the crime, and they do nothing to prevent the criminal re-offending. Supposedly 'tough' approaches to crime are, in fact, a soft option for both criminal and society: they let the former off the hook of accepting responsibility and making proper amends; and they let us off the hook of finding effective responses to the growing crime statistics. Mediation here, as elsewhere, is in its very early days, but it is pointing a way forward which deserves further exploration and a more serious commitment of resources.

* * *

The growing use of mediation within schools, communities and the criminal justice system is of symbolic as well as immediate and practical significance. It is also testimony to those social pioneers who are prepared to experiment, and fail, and try again just as experimenters have always done. The difference is that while the processes of human relations are just as complicated as those of atoms and molecules, we seem more reluctant to invest in understanding the former. The frustration is that we know mediation works when it is done well in appropriate cases. Even in neighbourhood mediation, in some ways the most difficult of all, in well over 70 per cent of cases there is some improvement in the situation or an actual agreement is reached.

Community mediation is important because it points the way to our social future. If we teach children to mediate and resolve conflict in schools, use the process to encourage them to accept responsibility when they offend, and provide every community with the resources to resolve its own disputes, then we will have to spend less money on defending ourselves against each other, and we will be able to invest more in creating a truly civil society.

CONTACTS

Mediation UK is the umbrella body for most community, victim/

offender and school mediation projects in the United Kingdom. It publishes a quarterly magazine, and regular newsletters containing details of mediation services, courses and workshops in the United Kingdom and around the world. It also publishes the *Directory of Mediation and Conflict Resolution Services, Guide to Starting a Community Mediation Service,* and its invaluable *Training Manual in Community Mediation Skills.*

Mediation UK
 82a Gloucester Road, Bishopston, Bristol BS7 8BN, Tel: 0117 241 234, Fax: 0117 441 387

Chapter 20

Alternative Futures

The purpose of this final chapter is to look briefly at the present and peer into the future. In mid-1995, the present is dominated to some extent by the need to absorb *Access to Justice* and Lord Woolf's recommendations for the expanded use of ADR within the civil justice system. An Interim Report of nearly three hundred pages is not going to be everyone's bedside reading, and it will mainly be read by ADR practitioners and lawyers. If you are interested in where ADR may go in the future, it is worth knowing that Lord Woolf writes as clearly as he thinks. It is a good read.

ACCESS TO JUSTICE **AND ADR**

As I have mentioned earlier, the ADR community has on the whole welcomed *Access to Justice*. Some of us regret the reluctance to at least pilot more court-annexed mediation schemes, or even a multi-door court scheme where litigants can choose whichever traditional or ADR process is most appropriate to their cases. Others believe that slow progress is better than none, and much better than being lost in the maze of other reforms he recommends. For all of us, this Report is a landmark in the development of ADR, and has done much to increase our confidence that we will not be voices crying in the legal wilderness for much longer: providing, of course, that its recommendations are implemented.

What exactly does he recommend in relation to ADR? For those who do not wish to read the whole thing, I am reproducing here his recommendations as they appear in Chapter 18 of the report:

1. Developments abroad, particularly those in the United States, Australia and Canada, in relation to ADR should be monitored, the Judicial Studies Board giving as much assistance as is practicable in relation to this exercise.
2. The retail sector should be encouraged to develop private ombudsman schemes to cover consumer complaints similar to those which now exist in relation to service industries; the government should facilitate this.
3. The relationship between ombudsmen and the courts should be broadened, enabling issues to be referred by the ombudsman to the courts and the courts to the ombudsman with the consent of those involved.
4. The discretion of the public ombudsmen to investigate issues involving maladministration which could be raised before the courts should be extended.
5. In the review of legal aid, the funding of voluntary organisations providing mediation services should be considered.
6. The courts should encourage and facilitate mini-trials in appropriate cases and use of mini-trials should be tested on an experimental basis in a selected number of courts.
7. The courts should, where appropriate, consider taking advantage of bodies such as the City Disputes Panel, to give authoritative guidance on particular practices from those who have experience at the highest level.
8. Where there is a satisfactory alternative to the resolution of disputes in court, use of which would be an advantage to the litigants, then the courts should encourage the use of this alternative: for this purpose, the staff and the judiciary must be aware of the forms of ADR which exist and what can be achieved.
9. At the case management conference and pre-trial review the parties should be required to state whether the question of ADR has been discussed and, if not, why not.
10. In deciding on the future conduct of a case, the judge should be able to take into account the litigant's unreasonable refusal to attempt ADR.
11. The Lord Chancellor and the Court Service should treat it as one of their responsibilities to make the public aware of the possibilities which ADR offers.
12. Considerations should be given to the way in which members

234

of the professions who are experienced in litigation and who retire at an early age, can be involved as 'civil magistrates' or otherwise, in support of the civil justice system.

As you can see, with the exception of the last recommendation and those relating to ombudsmen schemes, which are alternatives but not ADR in the stricter definitions of the field, Lord Woolf is giving ADR a fair wind. I have some reservations about recommendation 10, because although it may encourage ADR it could compromise the voluntary principle on which ADR rests, and Lord Woolf himself rejects elsewhere the idea of mandatory referrals to ADR.

How much significance can we attach to *Access to Justice*? It has to be said that the history of civil justice reviews is not encouraging; there has been one on average every 29 months for the past 150 years. However, it is widely acknowledged within the legal profession itself that something has to be done about civil litigation, and the immediate response to the Report has been generally positive – except among those whose livelihoods are most liable to be threatened by the diversion of smaller cases to ADR and Lord Woolf's other streamlining proposals. The expansion of ADR may provide some compensation for those who are prepared to make the leap.

BEYOND WOOLF

Let us look into the future. Could ADR at some point on the far horizon be more than just an alternative to litigation? Let us be really brave. Could it ever be a substitute for our present civil legal system? And if this is, at least in theory, possible, would it also be desirable? Could the Alternative in ADR mean truly that: something qualitatively different from what we have at present? Is it possible to have a dispute resolution system anchored in mediation and reconciliation rather than adjudication?

Let us assume, for the sake of exploration, that it would be possible to have a system based on the use of mediation as a first resort, with the panoply of law and adjudication in the supporting role. Would it be desirable? In that people would have to accept primary responsibility for sorting out their own problems, and therefore also for their own actions, it might have some very positive social benefits in addition to the personal ones. In that it might lead people to be a good deal more sensitive to the needs and aspirations of others, and generally learn through direct experience the merits of co-operation rather than confrontation, it sounds a rather cheerful prospect.

Will this happen? Probably not, but the reason for pursuing such a line of thought is the same reason that mediators use brainstorming. Playing with wild ideas is an excellent way to stir up old ones and generate new ones. For example, it suggests to me that ADR should always aim to deliver a qualitative difference in its approach to disputes. It also suggests that while ADR will need and should accept support from the legal profession for the time being, it must wherever possible develop and grow independently if this commitment to qualitative difference is to be preserved.

The first evidence for this independent growth will be the drawing of a firm dividing line between adjudicatory and non-adjudicatory processes. This leads to the conclusion that arbitration, summary hearings, private judging, ombudsmen and perhaps even mini-trials, are in time going to have to be clearly distinguished from processes such as mediation, neutral fact-finding and consensus-building. There will come a moment when an umbrella term such as ADR is a hindrance and a source of confusion if it continues to include the adjudicatory and non-adjudicatory, the adversarial and the collaborative.

This brainstorming approach to ADR's stand-alone potential generates a further question. What fundamental changes would there have to be in society at large for a dispute resolution system based on mediation rather than adjudication to function effectively? Would we first have to escape from the general 'adversarial assumption'? The adversarial assumption is, after all, a polite term for the law of the jungle – winner takes all and loser gets eaten – which is the basis on which most of the world operates. Perhaps for ADR to develop to its full potential we are going to have to overcome our almost universally adversarial social culture in which there is this unconscious assumption that conflict is inevitable, and that if it cannot be avoided, then it must be won or lost.

Yet there is a danger of throwing the baby out with the bathwater, because the adversarial assumption also has its uses. First, without it, could we distinguish right from wrong? Second, there are some wrongs that have to be opposed with all our energy: there are some issues towards which a more consensual approach would be tantamount to collusion. Third, there are times when the adversarial approach is imperfect but preferable to the alternatives. We are back to the problem that because the adversarial assumption is so ingrained, and so powerfully reinforced by the way most of our institutions operate, it tends to be used even when it is inappropriate.

The replacement of the automatic adversarial assumption with collaborative or consensual assumptions where appropriate would really make a difference not only to the future of ADR, but in the world generally. Is this remotely possible? One's first answer is 'No – not a hope.' But every age holds beliefs that subsequent generations find ridiculous. A century ago travel through air and space were the stuff of science fiction. Fifty years ago, smallpox was inevitable; it has since been eradicated. Five years ago people were still saying that mediation could never be used to resolve complex commercial disputes.

The major task for all of us involved in ADR in this generation is to challenge the adversarial assumption: to demonstrate that it is not inevitable any more than litigation is inevitable and the only way to deal with disputes. We have already started on this task. Every time people are helped to prevent a dispute through partnering we challenge the belief that disputes are inevitable. Every school which establishes a mediation programme to reduce bullying teaches children new ways to resolve conflict in the home, in the street, and later at work. Every business dispute mediated is an advertisement and an encouragement for the next business dispute to be resolved the same way.

If we can change our basic beliefs about how disputes can be resolved, then we will change the actions which follow from them. We have demonstrated that all sorts of disputes can be resolved consensually. We now have to persuade more people to use ADR methods, to learn from them, and to take that learning into the wider world. We will never get rid of disputes, but we can prevent some, cut the costs of others, and in the process contribute to creating a marginally saner society.

Appendix A: Sample Agreement to Mediate

I am grateful to ADR Group and IDR Europe Ltd for permission to reproduce their standard 'Agreement to Mediate'.

AGREEMENT TO MEDIATE

NAMES: ————————————————————————————
hereby agree to have IDR Europe Ltd. administer the mediation of their dispute concerning:

————————————————————————————————

on the following terms and conditions:

1. Mediation Procedures

The mediation shall be held and conducted according to this Agreement to Mediate and the current Mediation Procedures of IDR Europe Ltd. attached hereto and incorporated herein.

2. Mediator

The parties agree that———————————— will be the Mediator. The parties recognise that the Mediator is an independent contractor and not an agent or employee of IDR Europe Ltd.

3. Mediation Fees

a) The Mediation fee with be £———— for a minimum of five hours; an additional fee of £———— /hour/party will be charged thereafter, both plus VAT. Mediator travel time and expenses will be charged at Law Society rates. Incidental expenses at cost. The parties agree to repay Mediation fees as follows:

Amount ——————————————
Payable by ——————————————
Amount ——————————————
Payable by ——————————————

and the parties understand that the Mediation Session will not take place until such fees are prepaid as provided for.

b) Any charges for Mediation Fees in excess of the amount on deposit shall be paid within seven days in equal proportions or, if agreed otherwise, in such other proportions as the parties have agreed. The Mediator's expenses and travel time shall be paid in accordance with IDR Europe Ltd policy. At the conclusion of the mediation, after deduction of the administrative fee, the fee for the Mediator's time and the reimbursement of expenses, any unused prepaid Mediation Fees will be promptly returned to the parties in the proportions in which they were prepaid.

4. Consulting with Legal Advisers

Any party not represented by a legal adviser or in appropriate cases other professional adviser is advised to consult one before, during and after the Mediation Session and before finalising an agreement reached pursuant to the Mediation. The parties recognise that neither IDR Europe Ltd nor the Mediator is giving legal advice or acting as a lawyer for any of the parties or analysing or protecting any party's legal rights.

5. Private Sessions

The Mediator may hold private sessions with only one party. These private sessions are designed to improve the Mediator's understanding of the party's position. Information gained by the Mediator through such a session is confidential unless (a) it is in any event publicly available or (b) the mediator is specifically authorised by that party to disclose it.

6. Confidentiality

(a) The parties recognise that the Mediation Session is for the purpose of attempting to achieve a negotiated settlement and as such all information provided during the Mediation Session is without prejudice and will be inadmissable in any litigation or arbitration of the dispute. Evidence which is otherwise admissible shall not be rendered inadmissible as a result of its use in the Mediation Session. The parties will not subpoena or otherwise require IDR Europe Ltd or the Mediator or any other person attending the mediation under the auspices of IDR Europe Ltd to testify or produce records, notes or any other information or material whatsoever in any future or continuing proceedings.

(b) All documents, statements, information and other material produced or given for or during the Mediation whether in writing or orally, shall be held in confidence by the parties and shall be used solely for the purposes of the Mediation. At the termination of the Mediation all such material shall be returned to the originating party or forthwith destroyed at their option.

7. Termination of Mediation Session

Either of the parties or the mediator shall be entitled in their absolute discretion to terminate a Mediation Session at any time without giving any reason therefor.

Name:——————————   Name:——————————————
Address:——————————   Address:—————————————
——————————————————————————
——————————————————————————
Date: ————————————   Date:—————————————————
Signed:——————————   Signed:—————————————————

Accepted to administer the mediation as provided for:—
Date: ——————————————————
Signed: ———————————————
      IDR Europe Ltd

Appendix B: Sample Mediation Clause

This mediation clause is recommended by one of the United Kingdom's ADR providers. I suggest that before using it in a contract, you check with your legal advisers that it is appropriate to do so.

Any dispute or difference between the parties arising out of or in connection with this agreement shall first be referred to mediation in accordance with the mediation procedures of [*insert the name of your proposed mediation provider*].

The mediator shall be agreed upon by the parties and failing such agreement within 15 (fifteen) days of one party requesting the appointment of a mediator and providing their suggestion therefor, the mediator shall be appointed by the then President of the Law Society. Unless agreed otherwise the parties shall share equally the costs of the mediation.

The use of mediation will not be construed under the doctrine of laches, waiver or estoppel to affect adversely the rights of either party and in particular either party may seek a preliminary injunction or other judicial relief at any time if in its judgment such action is necessary to avoid irreparable damage.

This particular provider ends the clause with provision for a referral to arbitration should the mediation prove inconclusive.

Should the parties fail to reach agreement on their dispute or difference through the aforesaid mediation then the dispute or difference shall be referred to and finally resolved by arbitration under the Rules of the Chartered Institute of Arbitrators, which Rules are deemed to be incorporated by reference into this clause.

They also suggest the substitution of the London Court of International

Arbitration for the Chartered Institute of Arbitrators for agreements involving one or more non-UK parties.

Further Reading

Acland, Andrew Floyer (1990) *A Sudden Outbreak of Common Sense,* London: Hutchinson Business Books.

Bevan, Alexander (1992) *Alternative Dispute Resolution,* London: Sweet and Maxwell.

Centre for Dispute Resolution, *ADR Route Map: Working with ADR.*

Cornelius, Helena and Faire, Shoshana (1989) *Everyone Can Win,* Sydney: Simon and Schuster.

Crawley, John (1992) *Constructive Conflict Management,* London: Nicholas Brealey.

Carpenter, Susan and Kennedy WJD, (1988) *Managing Public Disputes,* San Francisco: Jossey-Bass.

Crum, Thomas (1987) *The Magic of Conflict,* New York: Simon and Schuster.

Davis, Gwynn and Roberts, Marian (1988) *Access to Agreement,* Milton Keynes: Open University Press.

De Bono, Edward (1986) *Conflicts,* London: Penguin.

Fisher, Roger and Ury, William (1986) *Getting to Yes,* London: Hutchinson Business Books.

Fisher, Thelma (ed. 1990) *Family Conciliation within the UK,* Bristol: Family Law.

Friend, John and Hickling, Allen (1987) *Planning Under Pressure,* Oxford: Pergamon.

Kennedy, Gavin (1989) *Everything is Negotiable,* London: Arrow Business Books.

Mackie, Karl (ed. 1991) *A Handbook of Dispute Resolution: ADR in Action,* London: Routledge.

Parkinson, Lisa (1986) *Conciliation in Separation and Divorce,* London: Croom Helm.

Susskind, Lawrence and Cruikshank, Jeffrey (1987) *Breaking the Impasse: Consensus Approaches to Resolving Public Disputes,* New York: Basic Books.

Ury, William (1991) *Getting Past No,* New York: Bantam.

Wright, Martin (1991) *Justice for Victims and Offenders,* Buckingham: Open University Press.

INDEX